HOME

David Littlefield

HOME
INVESTING IN DESIGN

John Wiley & Sons, Ltd

Published in Great Britain in 2008 by
John Wiley & Sons Ltd

Copyright © 2008
John Wiley & Sons Ltd, The Atrium, Southern Gate,
Chichester, West Sussex PO19 8SQ, England
Telephone +44 (0)1243 779777

Email (for orders and customer service enquiries):
cs-books@wiley.co.uk
Visit our Home Page on www.wiley.com

Other Wiley Editorial Offices
John Wiley & Sons Inc., 111 River Street,
    Hoboken, NJ 07030, USA
Jossey-Bass, 989 Market Street, San Francisco,
    CA 94103-1741, USA
Wiley-VCH Verlag GmbH, Boschstr. 12,
    D-69469 Weinheim, Germany
John Wiley & Sons Australia Ltd, 42 McDougall Street,
    Milton, Queensland 4064, Australia
John Wiley & Sons (Asia) Pte Ltd, 2 Clementi Loop #02-01,
    Jin Xing Distripark, Singapore 129809
John Wiley & Sons Canada Ltd, 5353 Dundas Street West,
    Suite 400, Etobicoke, Ontario M9B 6H8, Canada

Wiley also publishes its books in a variety of electronic formats.
Some content that appears in print may not be available in
electronic books.

Executive Commissioning Editor: Helen Castle
Project Editor: Miriam Swift
Publishing Assistant: Calver Lezama

ISBN   978-0-470-51672-0

Cover design and layouts by Liz Sephton
Printed and bound by Printer Trento, Italy

Contents

158 Primer

Introduction

Engaging a designer to reinvent your home is not something that should be undertaken lightly. Contemporary architects and designers have a knack of creating spaces that look easy; clean lines, built-in services, fine details and canny space-saving techniques can be combined to create a home that looks as if it was always meant to be that way. The best design often looks effortless, obvious even. But the houses and apartments featured in this book have generally been far from easy to create, and the investment in design has been one of effort as well as money.

This book tells the stories that often go untold. It is about the processes that led to the design, rather than the design itself. In these pages clients recount how they first came to believe that the intervention of an architect might be a good idea, and their tales unfold to reveal how the architect was chosen, how the design advanced and how the builder managed to turn the drawings into a built reality. Architects describe how they responded to a given brief and helped a client turn a vague aspiration into something that improved their lives. In the 17 cases that follow (some expensive indulgences, others incredible examples of value for money), both clients and architects demonstrate the level of commitment required on a building project. Extending or reinventing your home can be an exciting challenge, and any client can expect a medium-sized project to last two years from planning to completion. Inevitably, there will be setbacks and moments of despair but as the projects in the following pages demonstrate, it will always be worth the effort. All of the case studies presented here have given people more space, better light, improved facilities and a good deal of flexibility; and quite apart from these very practical benefits, they are often beautiful and uplifting.

The book is divided into two parts: the case studies, followed by a series of primers explaining the broad principles of design and the architectural process. This book is intended to be practical as well as inspirational. It shows what is possible if homeowners think carefully, ask plenty of questions and form a close bond with a design professional.

case studies

detached houses

Transformation of a farm building, Somerset

SUMMARY OF WORKS	Complete reinvention of original building; two-storey extension
HOUSE DESCRIPTION	Detached 19th century dwelling in rural location
CONTRACT VALUE	Unknown ('a lot,' admits the client)
TIME PERIOD (planning through to completion)	4 years
RESULT	An extraordinary reimagining of a poor quality and shabby farm building into luxury accommodation
ARCHITECT	Charlotte Skene Catling

This award-winning rebuild and extension to a 19th-century cheese factory and cottage is a salutary example of what can be achieved when you mix an enlightened client, talented architect, generous funding and time. The complete reinvention and rethinking of what was once a rather shabby rural building honours the site through a careful contemplation of materials and craft. To be in this house is a moving experience, and that has just as much to do with the materials and the way they have been put together as with the spaces themselves – in fact, space and materiality become the same thing.

The house was built by the client's great-great-grandfather on the family estate. The building had ceased to be used for cheese making by the 1960s and instead provided housing for tenant farmers. By the late 1990s it had become shabby and in severe need of modernising – it had poor heating and little insulation. Niall Hobhouse, an art dealer who manages the estate on behalf of his family, commissioned architect Charlotte Skene Catling, a family friend, to consider bringing the building up to modern standards. But the project hadn't progressed far when Hobhouse realised that it could become far more interesting than originally envisaged. At this point, he began to consider living in it himself.

Significantly, Hobhouse had very particular ideas about how to approach the project. He neither wanted to gentrify it ('The last thing I wanted to do was take a piece of second-rate housing and put a pediment on it,' he says) or make a dramatic statement. Rather, clues were to be taken from the local context and used to drive a scheme that would be almost unique in every detail. 'It would have been frankly cheaper and simpler to knock the house down and start again. But

opposite At night this oak and glass extension glows like a Chinese lantern. The pool cuts into the house, and can be accessed from either side from a pair of bathrooms.

top North elevation of the
development by Charlotte Skene
Catling, taken through a section of
landscape. The position of the small
swimming pool can be seen in the
centre of the drawing.

above South elevation of the
scheme, showing the original
house and the landscape beyond.
From this position the new
addition is hidden from view.

left and above During
daylight hours, the extension
appears a relatively humble
structure – almost barn-like.
The client was anxious that the
design revealed little of the bold
spaces within.

below The house meets an
embankment, shown here,
retained by locally quarried
stone. Openings are created
with slabs of welded steel.

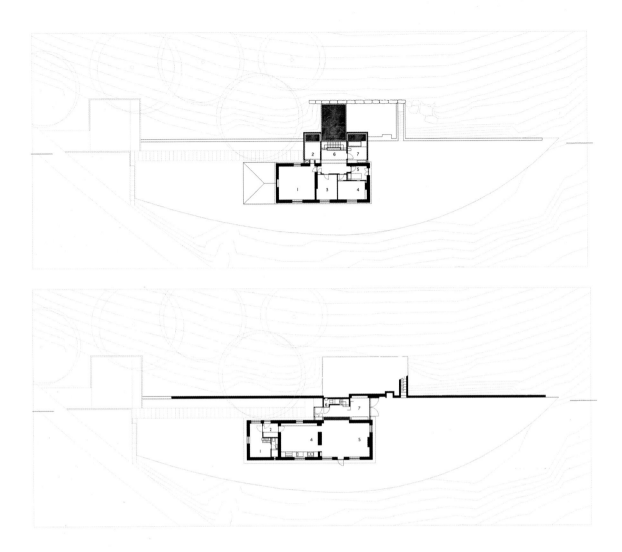

that wasn't what I wanted to do,' says Hobhouse. 'The decision was to take the existing house as a given – as already part of the landscape. My whole position on architecture is that it should be all about landscape. All architecture should take landscape as its starting point.'

Although the two-storey house was not demolished, it was fairly comprehensively taken apart – the roof was replaced, the ceilings were raised and the floors lowered. A great chunk of wall to one side was also removed, to make way for an oak and glass extension, which provides a new entrance, circulation and bathroom facilities. This extension, which nestles into a bank of earth, could more accurately be described as a piece of architectural furniture rather than as a building. As its design

progressed, Hobhouse and Skene Catling realised that the project was becoming too complex for the builders employed on the Hadspen Estate, where the house is situated. Client and architect sourced a range of local

top First-floor plan. The elevated spaces of the extension can now be seen, including the pool (top centre) flanked by a pair of baths.

above Ground-floor plan. The principal approach is from the left, along a wall banked up against the earth.

opposite Through a channel, with the house to the right and an embankment to the left, lies the main approach to the house. The wall to the left is made of breezeblocks.

opposite and left Close up, one can see that the facade of the extension is not composed of timber slats. Rather, it is constructed from lengths of oak separated by sheets of glass.

below Inside the house, the oak is planed and appears much less rustic than it does externally. The structure was created by a cabinet-maker who cut the timber, erected it temporarily in the workshop in order to test it, and then disassembled it before moving it to the site.

contractors and specialists including a cabinet-maker to produce the oak frame, and a stonemason to fashion vast slabs of Indian slate into worktops, flooring and baths.

Even then, the path from inception to completion was not an easy one: 'I knew what I was getting, but it turned out to be very difficult to get it,' says Hobhouse. Skene Catling would exasperate the builders by demanding a level of detail that they simply weren't used to producing, and the relationship between client and architect became

strained at times. 'Charlotte really, really wanted to get it right, but the difficulty she had was that I'm a very hands-on client. We have battled it out. But to be fair, neither of us knew what we were taking on. At the end we were both exhausted,' remembers Hobhouse.

Just about all building projects contrive to be more complex than imagined. This development turned out to be trickier than most because not only is it non-standard in almost every respect, it is also experimental. The

left The gap between the original 19th-century house and the new addition is clearly expressed with a steel and glass slot 450 millimetres (17.5 inches) wide.

opposite The kitchen. Large slabs of Indian slate form elegant and extremely hardwearing work surfaces.

walls of the extension are composed of thick planks of oak – reminiscent of the stacks of timber drying out in nearby barns – separated by sheets of glass laid flat on top of each other. In fact, the architect persuaded the glass manufacturer, Pilkington, to donate the glass free of charge because the technique was so original. This is no ordinary oak frame, and the external edges even retain the bark in many places. It is an alluring object; it is tempting to describe this extension as 'rustic', but the term fails to capture the finesse and innovation, which become apparent up close. Hobhouse's brief was to create a building that was not 'self-consciously radical', at least from the outside – the resolution of the extension has worked because at a distance it has something of a farmyard lean-to about it. It is only when stood inside that the full drama of this project reveals itself.

The original building has been configured largely with kitchen and living space on the ground floor, with bedrooms above. The extension, separated from the host building by a steel and glass slot, contains a pair of bathrooms, which begin to wrap around an external pool that pushes into the earth bank. In spite of its ambition, the project easily gained planning permission in May 2002 but it took four more years to complete. 'Was it worth it? That's an unqualified yes,' says Hobhouse. 'It really is an incredibly liveable house, and I've definitely learned something about how I want to live.'

left The interior of the original house (a cheese-making factory and cottage) has also been entirely remade. White walls and wide oak floorboards provide a rich yet broadly neutral backdrop to the client's furniture collection.

below One of the bedrooms contains a mezzanine-level space in the roof, providing extra storage and a spare sleeping area. These steps up to this unexpected zone double up as storage.

Extension and improved layout to a 1960s house, Berkshire

SUMMARY OF WORKS	Two-storey extension, reworking of entrance and kitchen
HOUSE DESCRIPTION	Detached 1960s house
CONTRACT VALUE	£200,000
TIME PERIOD (planning through to completion)	22 months
RESULT	A more efficient house, freed of many problems. Much improved spaces
ARCHITECT	Alastair Howe Architects

This house, built in 1962, is the epitome of its time. With its flat roof, expansive windows and dubious construction quality, the building was in need of some care and attention by the time Rex and Rikki Lucas bought it in 1996: 'We spent every penny we could on buying the house, so we couldn't really do anything with it,' says Rikki Lucas. 'Although we were conscious of the fact that the roof needed doing.'

The house had, in fact, been originally built as two semis but the individual dwellings had been knocked into one in the 1970s. At about the same time, a carport

had been given walls to form a new entrance and bedroom. It was all done rather clumsily; large panels of glass caused the rooms to overheat in the summer and haemorrhage heat in the winter. The timber walls of the building contained little or no insulation and, structurally, the house could be described as flimsy. But some of the spaces were expansive and the generous gardens and almost rural location are superb.

Things began to change for the Lucas family around 1998. Rex Lucas works in the electronics industry and much of his remuneration package was in shares – and at this time the value of the stock market, especially of the new dotcom businesses, was healthy and getting healthier. After much consideration the family decided to capitalise on its good fortune, demolish the house and replace it with something more robust and energy efficient.

opposite The front of the redeveloped house, with the new extension in the foreground. The timber cladding of the extension responds to the timber skin of the original 1960s building – but the recent work is far better insulated.

This decision was the start of an architectural odyssey. In spite of the Lucas family's inexperience in architectural matters, they did everything right. They contacted the Royal Institute of British Architects (RIBA), and drew up a list of architects, both local and London-based. They also bought the book *New Architects* published that year by the Architecture Foundation, from which they extracted a few more names to add to the list. They examined online portfolios at a time when the Internet was in its infancy, and interviewed architects over the phone. Some architects were invited to the house.

Eventually the Lucases selected Alastair Howe, partly because of his own merits and partly because other architects seemed to exclude themselves: 'I might be being unfair, but the impression I got from some of the people we interviewed was that they wanted to build something in their own image – something for their own greater glory,' says Rex Lucas, who was troubled by the egos of some of those on the short list. Others, however, made the assumption that the Lucases wanted something more traditional, along the lines of what the property ads call an 'executive home'. This put them right off.

Howe, on the other hand, actually liked the house that he was asked to consider demolishing. 'He did say that if we wanted a house like the [more conventional] one next door, we were talking to the wrong guy,' remembers Rex Lucas. Howe also boasted in the *New Architects* book that he had a reputation for keeping costs down and bringing projects in on time. He got the job.

left Night view. The extension can be seen on the right with the study on the ground floor and the new master bedroom above.

FOLLOWING PAGES

left The join between the new and the old. The original house appears on the right side of the black 'seam' (an expansion joint). The extension, on the left, begins with a glazed link.

right The original spiral staircase. Different design schemes proposed moving the stairs from the hall, but eventually it remained where it has always been. The opening through the kitchen beyond is new.

This is a story of many twists and turns, but the climax is this: after arriving at a highly contemporary design; after securing planning permission; after neglecting to maintain the original building; after moving into rented accommodation; after commissioning a demolition crew – the stock market crashed. The Lucas family were literally two days away from having their house torn down and unable to pay for its replacement. It was a close shave. Instead of building the house of their dreams, Rex and Rikki Lucas commissioned a local builder to repair and patch up the house where needed and they moved back in. Fortunately, they hadn't bothered with a house wrecking party, to the annoyance of their teenage son.

All this was a great shame because Howe had worked hard over many months to generate a scheme (via bubble diagrams, sketches and frequent site visits) that captured the spirit of the original house, while building to contemporary standards and making best use of the landscape and the light. It was an ambitious scheme, one that had grown in scale and complexity during the design process. Originally budgeted at £400,000, the Lucases began to add things to the original brief (a basement, for example), and when Howe warned that their budget was going to be sorely tested, Rikki and Rex didn't react negatively. Howe took this as a sign that the original budget was indicative only, and the cost of the house he was designing gradually crept up to £600,000, finally settling at around twice the original budget. In spite of some misgivings over price, the Lucases accepted the final design, as did their neighbour who, thanks to a restrictive covenant, also needed to consent to the proposal.

After the stock market crash towards the end of 2000, Howe quickly sketched two or three cheaper alternatives, but such was the economic uncertainty of the time that the Lucases had no real alternative but to abandon the project altogether. Howe didn't hear from them for two and a half years. When the Lucases called in mid-2003, they had a clearer idea of how he could

opposite The en suite bathroom adjacent to the new master bedroom is a minimal affair – cooler and more enclosed than other spaces within the house. The bath becomes an object rather than a mere appliance.

right The 1960s timber panelling inside the house has been retained. New paving slabs have been used on the floor.

right The windows in the extension are deliberately smaller than those of the original house. This is part of a strategy to control heat and light levels more effectively.

help. The budget was a more modest £200,000 and the job was to extend the house and make the original building function more effectively. Much of the house remains untouched, to be attended to at a later stage, but it has gained a more generous entrance hall, which now connects directly to a refitted kitchen. There is also a two-storey extension providing a ground-floor shower room and study, and a first-floor master bedroom adjacent to a showpiece bathroom. Bedroom number two has also been rebuilt, adding an en suite bathroom and a pair of insulated walls. Some structural brickwork has been replaced and guttering improved. The building is still recognisably the house that the Lucas family bought in 1996, but many of its major failings have been removed.

The centrepiece is the extension that replaces a garage. Curiously, this addition is structurally separate from the main house, which tends to move more than a well-built modern house should. The extension therefore, sits on a much firmer foundation than the house itself, and is joined to the original building via a flexible expansion joint. It even has its own boiler and heating system, as movements between the different parts of the house would have caused problems with the plumbing. In spite of this, the join between the original building and its extension is not obvious, and the use of materials,

above and right
Architect's sketches of the scheme, from three different viewpoints (from the drive, garden and rear), showing how the extension will sit with the 1960s house. The sketches are remarkably accurate, and compare well with the built form.

proportions and overall design language is such that Howe has created a building of a certain 'wholeness'. The new timber cladding responds to what was already there and costs were kept down by using outdoor paving slabs indoors (you would never know), and by customising (as is often the case) IKEA kitchen cabinets for a bespoke look.

The main attraction is the suite of rooms surrounding the master bedroom. The bedroom itself is not vast, but it doesn't need to be. What was once the main bedroom is now a walk-in wardrobe accessed via the short, glass-topped link between the original building and the new extension. The bathroom contains an enormous sculptural bath, which describes a wonderful ellipse in the centre of the room: 'This is about the only thing that survives from our very original plans,' says Rikki Lucas.

The house still needs work but not urgently. In particular, it could still do with the long-planned louvres over the large south-facing windows, to better control summer heat and light. The addition of solar panels is being considered. These things can wait. In the meantime, this house can now function, as it should: 'With proper maintenance, there is no reason why this building should not last beyond a couple of hundred years,' says Alastair Howe.

below The four elevations of the house. Windows are picked out as grey panels.

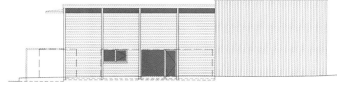

NORTH ELEVATION

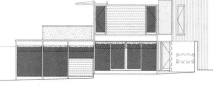

EAST ELEVATION

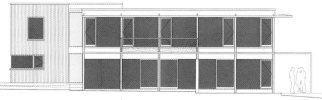

SOUTH ELEVATION

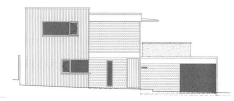

WEST ELEVATION

Extension and rescue of a village house, Hampshire

SUMMARY OF WORKS	Interior fit out; link to refurbished coach house; living room and bedroom extension
HOUSE DESCRIPTION	Detached Victorian villa
CONTRACT VALUE	£250,000
TIME PERIOD (planning through to completion)	20 months
RESULT	Transformation of poor quality, badly maintained house into a large and well-appointed family home
ARCHITECT	CaSA Architects

When Adam Dennes of CaSA Architects wrote the planning application statement for this project, he described the house as 'a plain and unexceptional Victorian villa'. It is something that clients Rob and Lizzie Baylis have never let him forget (no one wants to hear their home described like that), even if the architect was trying to maximise his chances of securing planning permission. The truth is it was probably a fair description.

Today, this house, in a rural location near Southampton, is far from plain and unexceptional. It has been intelligently extended and remodelled in a manner that shows contemporary design need not remove itself from

craft and sensitivity. A wide range of materials (timber, glass, lead, brick, Welsh slate and stainless steel) has been combined to cleverly update this house without challenging it. Aspects of this project, completed in 2002, are clearly recent additions but they manage to speak the language of modernity gently.

A key reason why this development worked so well was because the client already knew the architect – Dennes is the brother of a close friend. Dennes was relatively inexperienced when the Baylis family turned to him for advice on purchasing what was to be their first home: 'We liked all his ideas, and we sort of wanted to give him a break,' says Rob Baylis. So the client bought the house, built in 1857, largely on the strength of Dennes' recommendation – they didn't even bother with a survey. The fact that the building was clearly subsiding in one corner put no one off; indeed, it prompted Dennes to consider this portion of the house ripe for an extension, as building work would be necessary. The lack of central heating, poor electrical system and 'Dig for Victory' garden were similarly dismissed. The family moved in during August 1998 and, after 18 months of making the house fit for habitation, set Dennes to work in 2000.

The brief was all rather vague, partly because the clients had no firm ideas and partly because of the high degree of trust they invested in Dennes: 'We didn't really know what we wanted, although we did know that we wanted open-plan, contemporary living within a house that still felt old,' says Rob Baylis. 'Because we'd known Adam

for quite a long time, he had a pretty good idea of what we'd like and what we wouldn't like. He knew that space, light and colour were very important to us.'

And with a brief as scanty as that, they virtually let Dennes get on with it. 'They played a minimal role in the development of the building plans. They trusted me completely,' remembers Dennes. This level of trust was important and had a profound effect on the final outcome. At one stage, for example, the contractor proposed retaining an existing doorway rather than moving it as proposed by Dennes – the architect stuck to his guns, insisting that (regardless of the cost and effort involved) the position of the door was crucial

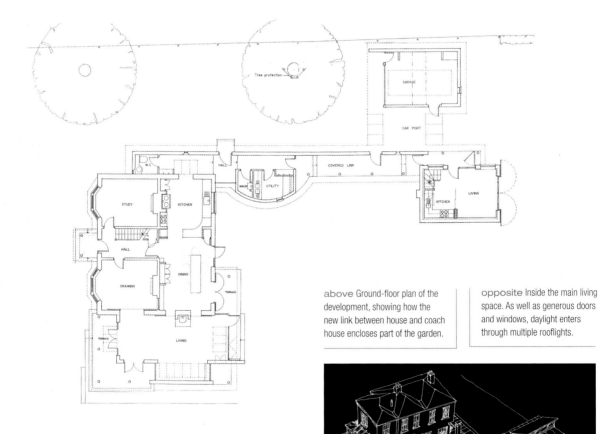

above Ground-floor plan of the development, showing how the new link between house and coach house encloses part of the garden.

opposite Inside the main living space. As well as generous doors and windows, daylight enters through multiple rooflights.

right Architect's sketch illustrating the major moves of the development – an extension to the living room, wrapping around the house, and a link between the main building and the coach house. A garage building, at 90 degrees to the link, received planning permission but was eventually built further back along the drive.

to the views, sightlines and control of movement that he envisaged. Dennes got his way and the clients now admit that he was right all along. Having said that, Dennes didn't spend their money willy-nilly. While on holiday in Australia, he noticed some light fixtures that were perfect for the Baylis house. At AU$350 apiece, they were nothing short of extravagant, so Dennes contacted the manufacturer and persuaded them to make a cheaper alternative; he returned to the UK with 25 affordable prototypes.

Soon after taking on this job, Dennes took up a position with Bath-based Martin Gledhill Architects (responsible for the extension to the thatched cottage described in the following case study) and Dennes and Gledhill ran the development jointly. The development comprised a number of components: to provide a link between the main building and a small coach house to the rear, which is used as accommodation for guests, and simultaneously enclose part of the large garden; extending the house to the side, creating a new living space and master bedroom suite above; and remodelling the interior. This project was conducted with an almost obsessive attention to detail: openings were carefully placed to provide subtle glimpses from room to room; the ceilings and skylights were very nearly sculpted to modulate the light to best effect; timber columns were set within bespoke 'headers' and 'footers' of steel; the sloping site was handled

deftly, via a series of overlapping flat roofs; the gutters drain through stainless-steel down pipes: 'I had the opportunity to really craft this building and love every detail,' says Dennes.

The selection of the builder was crucial. Unusually, Dennes did not put the job out to tender. This job was going to need the attentions of a careful builder, so making a selection on price alone would not have been sensible. Also, the clients preferred to use a local builder but, being based in Bath, Dennes had no experience of working with Hampshire contractors. After securing recommendations from local architects, Dennes drew up a short list of builders, interviewed them and even inspected their work. Once he had identified a favourite he negotiated a fixed price of £250,000.

By common consent it was a good choice. The build took longer than expected (about a year rather than nine months), but the work was conducted in such a manner that the clients and their two children did not have to move out. In spite of the complexity of the details, the work has been executed well and traditional materials,

above Night view of the link building, illustrating the clerestory windows and the way the roofline rises in a series of steps.

below View across the rear of the house, towards the curving wall of the utility room, located in the link. This image encapsulates a wide range of ideas and materials in the architect's palette – timber, stainless steel, lead, clerestory windows and fine carpentry.

such as timber and lead, have been fashioned in a way that is wholly contemporary. Unfortunately, this did result in one hiccup – one of the lead-covered flat roofs leaked. The leak, which was quickly fixed at no cost to the client, was the result of what Dennes calls 'a slightly unorthodox detail' and the fact that the main contractor undertook all the lead work himself. Dennes had assumed that the roofing would be subcontracted out to a more experienced, specialist lead worker; he insists the roof would have been watertight if this had been the case.

There is no harm done, and client–architect relations are as strong as ever. The Baylises are now considering a roof extension, adding a couple of bedrooms to this five-bedroom property: 'There is no doubt that the job will go to Adam,' says Rob Baylis.

left The new front door, positioned halfway along the link between main house and coach house. Glazing inside provides views right across the property, over the garden decking and into the living room on the far side.

below The rear of the house. The living room extension wraps around three sides of the house.

above Rear view of the completed kitchen extension. Inside the garden/courtyard, the construction material changes to timber.

following page Clerestory windows admit light from the roadside edge of the building, protecting privacy. Glazing becomes more generous on the garden side.

This listed cottage in Nettleton, Gloucestershire, could easily have been enlarged using the materials and design features of a bygone age; equally, the extension could have been wrought in a very contemporary language, going to great lengths to counterpoint the thatched original with the machined aesthetic of newness. Architect Martin Gledhill did neither. Instead, he worked on this building in much the same way as the people who constructed it over 300 years ago – by using good quality materials, many of them contemporary, and crafting them into a form that felt right.

Kitchen extension and other works to a thatched cottage, Gloucestershire

SUMMARY OF WORKS	Kitchen extension; refit of former kitchen as study; short link to out-building
HOUSE DESCRIPTION	Grade II listed cottage
CONTRACT VALUE	£85,000
TIME PERIOD (planning through to completion)	2 years
RESULT	Improved and expanded spaces for family with teenage children
ARCHITECT	Gledhill Walker Architects

Clients David and Helga Rhodes found their architect through a recommendation from a carpentry company. They liked him immediately: 'We wanted a very close working relationship with our architect and Martin welcomed this. We treated him like a friend and a member of the family. Martin is a very enthusiastic person and he demanded a lot of enthusiasm from us,' says David Rhodes. They also liked the way he quickly got to grips with the house and their half-formed brief, which involved replacing a small, cosy, dark kitchen with something larger and brighter.

What Gledhill did was completely rethink the project from first principles. While the client had imagined simply extending the kitchen by adding to the side of the house, Gledhill proposed moving the kitchen entirely – adding a new wing at right angles to the house and converting the old kitchen into a study. 'He listened carefully and was very aware of what we were trying to get at,' remembers David Rhodes. 'Within about 10 minutes Martin said, "OK, it should go here." We hadn't even thought of that.' This manoeuvre simultaneously enclosed part of the garden, creating a more intimate

courtyard space and screened one side of the house from the road. The reworking of the brief also informed the glazing strategy: on the roadside, windows are restricted to clerestories, allowing light to enter at a high level while preventing views in from passers-by; as the extension meets the house, the windows drop down slightly and glazing is added to the roof, allowing more daylight to penetrate into the adjacent living room; on the private garden side, however, glazing is generous.

Gledhill approached the local planning department very early on in the design process – as the cottage is listed, he needed to get the conservation officer on side before designs progressed too far. The conservation officer turned out to be highly supportive of the scheme, and even encouraged the mix of contemporary design and traditional materials: 'The use of materials and detailing needed to reflect a sense of care and permanence,' says the architect. 'The result is very much an amalgam of the creative dialogue between the local planning officers, the clients and ourselves.' The result is indeed an interesting design language – although thatch was never considered as a roofing material, the roadside wall

is made of stone found on site. Other building materials include oak, glass and lead, while water from the gutters flows down chains rather than down pipes. Completed in 2003, the project won an RIBA Town and Country Award the following year.

The motivation for changing the house in the first place was that the Rhodes family (all five of them) were beginning to feel cramped. The property's circulation was slightly awkward and spaces needed to be rationalised. Placing the kitchen in a new wing, adjacent to the living room, suited the way this family actually lived. Gledhill also converted a pantry into a bathroom and installed a short link between the house and an old outbuilding, now a teenager's bedroom. The architect also worked very closely with Helga Rhodes on

below Elevations of the cottage and extension, showing how the addition encloses the garden, forming a courtyard.

bottom Elevation of the cottage and kitchen extension, showing how the development appears from the roadside. The image illustrates the contemporary lines of the new addition as it emerges to the right of the building.

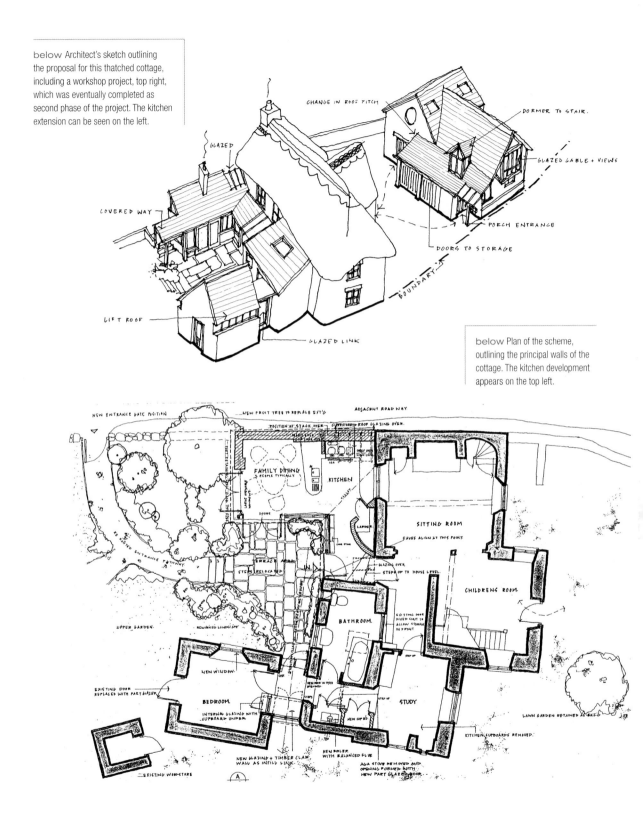

below Architect's sketch outlining the proposal for this thatched cottage, including a workshop project, top right, which was eventually completed as second phase of the project. The kitchen extension can be seen on the left.

CHANGE IN ROOF PITCH

DORMER TO STAIR.

GLAZED GABLE + VIEWS

GLAZED

COVERED WAY

PORCH ENTRANCE

DOORS TO STORAGE

BOUNDARY

LIFT ROOF

GLAZED LINK

below Plan of the scheme, outlining the principal walls of the cottage. The kitchen development appears on the top left.

NEW ENTRANCE GATE POSITION

NEW FRUIT TREE TO REPLACE EXT'G

ADJACENT ROAD WAY

POSITION OF STAIR OVER

CLERESTORY ROOF GLAZING OVER.

FAMILY DINING

KITCHEN

SITTING ROOM

EAVES ALIGN AT THIS POINT

DOORS

LADDER

TERRACE

STEPS RELOCATED

GLAZING OVER TO

STEPS UP TO HOUSE LEVEL.

CHILDRENS ROOM.

UPPER GARDEN.

REWORKED LANDSCAPE

BATHROOM.

EXISTING DOOR FEED CHUTE TO ALLOW STORAGE IN FRONT

STEP UP

NEW WINDOW.

EXISTING DOOR REPLACED WITH PART GLAZED

BEDROOM

INTERNAL GLAZING WITH CUPBOARD UNDER.

STUDY

STEP UP

NEW CUPBD

LAWN GARDEN RETAINED AS EXT'G

KITCHEN CUPBOARDS REMOVED.

EXISTING WOODSTORE

NEW GLAZING + TIMBER CLAD WALL AS INFILL LINK

NEW BOILER WITH BALANCED FLUE

AGA STOVE REMOVED AND OPENING FORMED WITH NEW PART GLAZED DOOR.

A

the design and specification of the kitchen, indeed, the layout of this space is almost entirely down to the client, who has put everything exactly where she wants it.

What works so well about this project is that, although it's clearly been well considered, it doesn't look as if anyone was trying too hard. The modern addition – more rigorously composed than the original – seems relaxed, while the cottage itself appears untroubled by what has happened. The ventilation stack above the Aga is suggestive of a chimney without actually having to be one (or pretending to be one). The fine lead work around the sills and roof edge is tight and contemporary. All this suited Helga Rhodes very much, who has an aversion to what she calls the 'clinical' lines of Modernism.

Often, though, this is an aesthetic that has to take its time, and Gledhill was frequently on site talking to builders about the resolution of specific details. It is not the standard architectural method these days, but Gledhill

above The oak letterbox sits within the stone wall as a small, discreet hatch.

below Chains replace down pipes from the gutters. When it rains, the disposal of water becomes a spectacle.

above The side of the development as completed. The 'chimney' is actually a cooker flue. Note the glazing between house and extension, which brings extra light deep into the original building.

prefers something of the master builder approach to architecture; not everything can be drawn in an office, remote from the project. To work properly, however, this strategy needs either builders with a very architectural sensibility or for the architect to be almost permanently present on site. Without the guiding hand of the architect, builders will generally revert to type and employ very conventional methods. For example, Gledhill specified a flat roof for the short link between the house and outbuilding but the builder installed it on a slight incline

for drainage reasons, making it appear plain wonky. Gledhill, having determined the incline was unnecessary for a roof of such a small size, had the builder refit the roof so that it appeared absolutely horizontal: 'I think he expects builders to share his enthusiasm for the build process,' says David Rhodes. Such was the clients' degree of satisfaction with Gledhill's approach to his craft that they commissioned him to design a new two-storey outbuilding, functioning as a workshop and B&B facility, which has since been completed.

Complete remodelling of a 1930s house, Oxfordshire

SUMMARY OF WORKS	Complete remodelling and extension, with loft conversion
HOUSE DESCRIPTION	Detached 1930s house
CONTRACT VALUE	£200,000
TIME PERIOD (planning through to completion)	19 months
RESULT	A doubling of accommodation
ARCHITECT	Spratley Studios

At the end of this ambitious project, this detached house emerged twice as large – growing from 139 to 279 square metres (1,500 to 3,000 square feet). Indeed, what was once a rather nondescript dwelling (highly typical of the 1930s), has been comprehensively rethought, remodelled and extended. So thorough is this intervention that one has to wonder why the client didn't simply knock the house down and start again. The answer is that the local planning authority would almost certainly not have approved a replacement house that could match the size of the extended one. Actually, the planning submission was for a house 2 metres (6.6 feet) bigger than the one shown here, but planning officers cautioned against such a vast expansion and the design was scaled back. The clients, Jon and Mel Watkins, now think the planners were right.

opposite The rear of the reinvented house. The first floor is clad in timber, while the ground floor, brick, makes way for a glazed box that can open up to the garden. Compare the extended roofline with the near point of the original house.

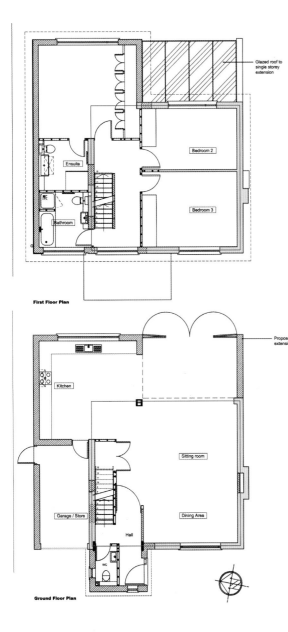

First Floor Plan

Glazed roof to single storey extension

Ensuite

Bedroom 2

Bathroom

Bedroom 3

proposed roof plan

Proposed new rooflight

Dormer window

Bedroom 4

Dormer window

Kitchen

Proposed 'lean-to' extension

Sitting room

Garage / Store

Dining Area

Hall

WC

Ground Floor Plan

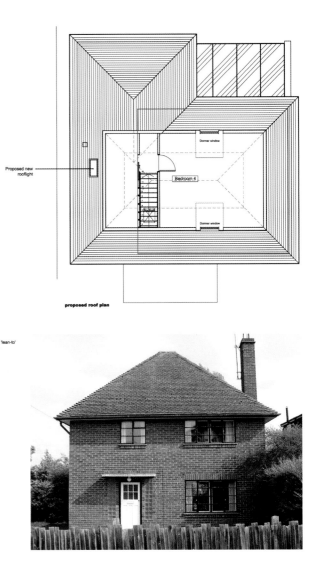

above Plans showing the extent of Spratley Studios' work to this house in Henley-on-Thames. The ground floor is shown bottom left, the first floor top left and the loft conversion top right. The red lines indicate the perimeter of the original house.

above, right The house as purchased by the clients, prior to the intervention of Spratley Studios. The house was basic, bland and utilitarian.

Jon Watkins is a project manager in the construction industry, so this job is not a typical one. The architects, Spratley Studios, were paid a lump sum to take the development up to the stage at which planning permission was granted, and they were then paid by the hour as and when they were needed. Watkins ran the project and employed a contractor run by his father. The completed project represents extraordinary value for money. Watkins bought the house in 2005 for £375,000 and the redevelopment cost around £200,000. The house is now valued at around £1million.

This project margin is not just down to the skill of Watkins as a project manager, but to the entire approach

left Bathroom facility in the loft, which also contains a generous new bedroom. Fixtures and fittings are elegant, yet inexpensive – a purchasing strategy which defines this project.

of the architect, Jeremy Spratley: 'Architecture need not be expensive or bespoke,' he says. 'An architect can help you see what you can't see for yourself, and that's where we add value. In this development we've done what we can with standard components, so much of what is here can be bought at a builder's merchant. There's nothing groundbreaking here. Only when it's been really worth it have we bought some one-offs, like bespoke pieces of glass.'

Spratley describes the original house as 'tatty and terrible'. Rooms were small and even though there were three bedrooms, two of them were tiny. Now the house boasts a ground floor dining/living/kitchen area, which is no less than vast, thanks to some clever structural engineering that enabled walls to be removed in the search for expansive, free-flowing space. A glazed box at the rear prevents this large interconnected room from becoming too dark. One of the most delightful spaces is the loft conversion where a large guest bedroom and bathroom have been created. Looking at the plans of the house best conveys the extent of the changes: at ground-floor level the entire rear wall has come down; and a rear corner of the house has been taken out over two storeys. Remarkably, a staircase has been inserted up to the loft room without making the landing feel too congested.

In design terms, Watkins gave Spratley something of a free rein (in fact, many of the details and design tactics are based on the architect's own home, which prompted Watkins to give him the job in the first place). The brief was fairly open and aspirational, and the only specific requirement from the client was that the house should become bigger, lighter and more open. The builder (Watkins' father), needed to be convinced about some of the things he was asked to do: full-height doors, which give a greater sense of the floor to ceiling height; shadow gaps; and cedar boarding as cladding for the outside of the house. On each count, once it was in place, the builder conceded that the architect was right all along. During the 18-month build period the clients moved out, but they lent a hand on site when they could. 'There were a few "tricky moments",' admits Spratley, 'such as replacing the roof in February. But generally the build went smoothly.'

The design language is warm and contemporary, with splashes of colour to enliven the whites, creams, limestone tiles and pale timbers of the fit out. But in spite of the finesse, it was a very nuts-and-bolts project: 'We have a very practical approach to our work,' says Spratley. 'You have to have a real understanding of what a builder can do. Other than that, you need a decent measured survey, a sense for how the proposed space relates to key services, and a special regard for planning policy. After that comes the art. It's a very nice thing to be able to make a swan out of an ugly duckling.'

opposite Seating area under the glazed box. This area is crucial for admitting natural light and preventing a very large floor space from becoming dark and gloomy.

above The kitchen area of the completed house, looking out to the rear garden.

Extension and reconfiguration of a 1970s house, Somerset

SUMMARY OF WORKS	Internal remodelling and extension
HOUSE DESCRIPTION	Detached 1970s house
CONTRACT VALUE	£100,000
TIME PERIOD (planning through to completion)	8 months
RESULT	Greatly expanded and rationalised spaces and circulation
ARCHITECT	Hallett Pollard Hilliar

The present configuration of this house in Freshford, Somerset, is the result of a slow evolution of ad hoc improvements that culminated in a drastic (and unexpected) remodelling programme. In September 2002, homeowner Ken Birleson asked his architect friend Neil Pollard for advice on what he might do with a spare pair of French doors. This very casual request triggered a series of conversations that led to a £100,000 rebuild. Some of the house remains unchanged, but Pollard's reworking has not only extended the house but also made it far lighter and immensely more sensible.

Birleson bought the house new for £21,000 in 1974 and added a single-storey rear extension in 1980. For many years the house functioned as a typical family home, and space was not in short supply. It was, however, awkward. The kitchen was long, narrow and dark enough to need the lights on almost permanently; the dining room was small; a downstairs bedroom was accessed by walking up some stairs, and then down again; and the spectacular views to the rear of the house

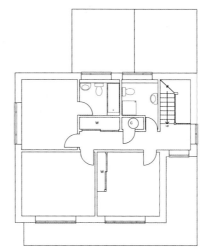

GROUND FLOOR PLAN   FIRST FLOOR PLAN

top row Plans (ground, left; first floor, right), showing the layout of this house prior to the architect's intervention.

bottom row These plans (ground, left; first floor, right) show the layout of the house after remodelling. Significantly, a first floor projection has been built upon, adding to the first floor, while the staircase has been moved to the centre.

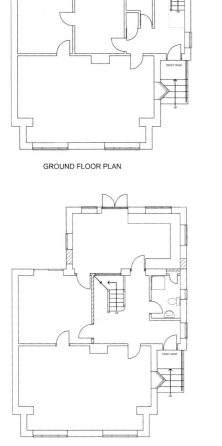

GROUND FLOOR PLAN   FIRST FLOOR PLAN

right A new skylight set atop the moved staircase brings light into the centre of the house, where it was formerly rather dark.

far right View from the new master bedroom to the rear of the property, which was formerly unseen from the top of the house.

were not available to any of the bedrooms. The entire house was a wasted opportunity.

'Before we could do anything, we had to resolve some of these problems,' says Neil Pollard, a director of Bath-based practice Hallett Pollard Hilliar. Instead of addressing each problem individually, Birleson, his late wife Jill and Pollard, looked for a 'total' solution that involved looking at the house afresh. A big part of the solution turned out to be moving the staircase from one side of the house into the centre. This bold gesture meant that daylight could enter more rooms directly, while the newly positioned staircase could be illuminated from above. The downstairs bedroom was then removed, allowing the kitchen to run along the full width of the house, freeing up space for the dining room to be widened. By building on top of the single-storey extension a new master bedroom could be added at the rear of the house, opening up the splendid views that had formerly been to the benefit of a pair of bathrooms. Over a number of weeks, through a process of conversation, sketching and resketching, a solution was reached. A planning application was made in February 2003.

The front of the house has changed little other than the addition of an overhanging roof to protect the approach to the front door. It is the centre and rear of the house that have been utterly transformed. The builder was found relatively easily. In the late 1990s the client had extended the living room by moving the front wall outwards, and the same builder was commissioned for this larger project. Scheduled to last for six months, the client decided to stay put: 'We lived rough,' says Birleson. 'We had no water for six weeks.'

The reinvention looks effortless, and the original lines of the house are virtually invisible. There is little or nothing to suggest that the house had ever looked any different. It was not easy, however; the roof required some clever structural gymnastics in order to fully resolve joining existing timberwork to the new upper storey.

What was once a fairly workaday and clumsy affair is now a home that draws light in to all the spaces that need it, while taking notice of its setting. Doors open directly on to the newly landscaped garden and each room has a proper regard for size, proportion and orientation. The success of the project can be put down to the same thing that characterises many of the projects described in this book: an open-minded client who has a positive and trusting relationship with the appointed architect. Typically, the solution to the problems suffered by this house did not present itself in a sudden flash of insight; rather, answers were arrived at in stages. Birleson even remembers enjoying the process,' It was quite a laugh,' he says.

Prior to the building work in 2003, the house was valued at £650,000; a valuation two years later put a figure of £780,000 on the building, easily covering the cost of the construction work. The client isn't tempted to sell, however, and he's already eyeing up a quiet corner at the rear of the house (faced by the dining room and kitchen), as a possible site for yet another phase of this house's almost constant reinvention.

Modernisation of a country cottage, Wiltshire

SUMMARY OF WORKS	Interior fit out
HOUSE DESCRIPTION	Detached cottage
CONTRACT VALUE	£40,000
TIME PERIOD (planning through to completion)	5 years
RESULT	Modernisation of a small cottage into a contemporary design statement
ARCHITECT	Griffiths Gottschalk

This detached house, tucked away out of sight in Bradford on Avon, occupies a slightly odd place in this book because the client–owner is also the architect. Contractual relationships do not feature in this case study, because there weren't any. The house appears here as an outstanding example of how a sensitive yet contemporary approach can be applied to an elderly building.

The property, originally a 16th-century weavers' cottage, was much smaller – literally a one-up, one-down dwelling with a pitched roof. In the 1820s the house doubled in size, when a very similar structure was added to one side. A flat-roofed, single-storey addition was built in the 1970s, adding kitchen, WC and bathroom space. John Griffiths, a skilled cabinet-maker as well as an architect, bought the house in 1999 for £128,000 and immediately set about undoing the damage of the preceding few decades: 'It was just awful. Everything was

opposite John Griffiths' house in Bradford on Avon. This building was constructed in three phases over a period of hundreds of years, ending in the single-storey extension (left) in the 1970s.

cheap,' he says. Moreover, because most of what he's done is cosmetic, and the house isn't listed, everything could be achieved without planning permission.

Over a five-year period Griffiths, who also runs the furniture design/making business Ooma Design, spent around £30,000 on the house and a further £10,000 on the garden. His strategy was to strip the house back to its original structure, to discover what had been covered up and remove all extraneous bits and pieces in an effort to get at the essence of the place. This involved removing plaster from the walls and then scraping pink paint from the stone beneath. The ceiling came down to reveal the timbers above. Niches were uncovered within the walls. Everything about the house has been remade with an obsessive attention to detail that is staggering. Even the 'twee and traditional' garden was almost entirely replaced in parallel with the house makeover.

below Griffiths' work as both architect and cabinet-maker is clearly seen. The floor, stairs and cupboard are of poplar, the table and bench of oak.

left In removing plaster from the walls, charming little niches were found beneath. These have been retained and put on view.

left The base of the stairs. The staircase is secured to a set of storage units with a steel pin.

opposite As the kitchen is located in the 1970s extension, Griffiths felt it appropriate to install a contemporary window. Sash windows are retained in older parts of the building.

left View from the kitchen through to the hall/diner. The level of the kitchen is considerably higher than the rest of the house due to the slope of the land on which the house is built.

Although the place has been treated with care, some of the building materials are surprisingly inexpensive. Much of the flooring and some of the furniture are made of poplar, a fast-growing, relatively soft hardwood with a wonderful grain and also good value for money. The kitchen is floored with concrete paving slabs that retailed at £1.50 each. Often, building projects should be judged in terms of how money is spent, rather than how much.

Griffiths says the key to unlocking the potential of a house like this is knowing how to look for clues, and letting the house guide you where appropriate: 'There has got to be a respect for the original building. There are clues in everything. You need to be sensitive to what is there, to be able to read it and discover what's relevant, and then to know when to push against it and when to play with it. It's these conscious choices which make a successful piece of work.'

During the construction work, most of which he undertook himself, Griffiths faced a number of dilemmas – such as whether or not to replace the sash windows with something more 21st century (he has fashioned

contemporary windows for the 1970s addition). After agonising, Griffiths settled on keeping them, albeit new replacements, because he felt a natural relationship had been established over the centuries between these structures and the surrounding stonework. And then he compares these windows with his new oak front door, in all its pared-back sleekness: 'You could argue that door is very modern, but actually it's very primitive. It's like a castle door. The sash windows are far more advanced, technologically, than the door. Sometimes old technologies retain validity. It all depends on context,' he says.

Griffiths has used a variety of different timbers in this house, each chosen for its role: iroko for kitchen and bathroom surfaces, including the bath, for its hardness,

above The living room. The box on the left, which swivels, contains audio-visual appliances.

right Living room with sofa. The influence of American artist and furniture-maker Donald Judd can be seen in Griffiths' work.

opposite First-floor study. The contemporary fit out in timber has a comfortable relationship with the elderly structure.

water resistance and deep colour; Californian yellow pine, selected for its visual warmth, has been used to clad the kitchen walls; oak has been used for specific pieces of furniture and doors; and poplar is found on the floor of the first-floor bedroom, replacing original elm boards that were too damaged to retain. Griffiths approaches design from a position of truthfulness to materials, purity of construction and simplicity of line. The fit out and furniture of this house, therefore, is put together in such a way that it complements the honesty and integrity of the buildings' original construction. Each piece – whether staircase, kitchen unit, bath fixture or door – has been designed and manufactured to emphasise the quality of the original house while being able to stand as an object in its own right. The result is a house of considerable authenticity; nothing pretends to be what it is not. Griffiths has created an interior

architecture of comfortable relationships, where the very new and the very old are at ease with one another.

At the time of writing, the house was on the market for £425,000, although Griffiths was not quite convinced that he should be selling it at all.

opposite When Griffiths bought the property in 1999, the house had conventional flat ceilings, obscuring the original timbers.

below, left The bath is made of iroko, an oily hardwood ideally suited to such a function.

below, right The WC is clad in Californian yellow pine. The space behind these boards is used to run services that would otherwise be on view. The same technique is used in the kitchen.

terraced and semi-detached houses

Extensive reworking of a large home, Wandsworth, south London

SUMMARY OF WORKS	Total reinvention of interior, plus extension in structural glass
HOUSE DESCRIPTION	Victorian semi-detached
CONTRACT VALUE	£500,000
TIME PERIOD (planning through to completion)	26 months
RESULT	Conversion of a multiple-occupancy house into a single, dramatic home
ARCHITECTS	The Pike Practice

When the client bought this 1890s semi in 2004, it was a building of flats and bedsits. Kitchens and bathrooms were everywhere. 'It was in a very poor condition. By the time we'd finished with it, there was not a single poor space in the house; prior to that, there wasn't a single decent one,' remembers architect Tom Pike, who isn't a fan of the exterior styling of this building, with its Dutch-style gables. 'But once inside, and you leave the facade behind, it's a completely different building. It's a different space; a different century.'

opposite The frameless structural glass can be seen at work here. Laminated glass strips provide ultra-modern beams.

Pike and the client have a business relationship that goes back several years. His practice was busy working on a scheme for a different house (a tricky loft conversion which won planning permission after a series of battles with the local authority) when the client decided to sell and buy this much larger property nearby. This was a different project entirely. 'We just gutted the place and got it back to the structure,' says Pike. The most ambitious element of the scheme is at the rear, where a section of the ground floor has been removed to allow people to peer down into the basement, where the kitchen-diner is now located. Above this two-storey space is a roof of structural glass, where laminated glass beams provide the structure as well as the canopy of this large, transparent box. At basement level the garden

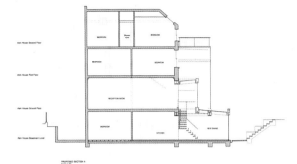

above Section through the house, showing the new glazed box and the balcony over the basement level.

right The basement-level kitchen, with living area above. Part of the ground floor was cut away to create this double-height space.

opposite This night view illustrates the degree to which the house has been opened up at the rear. 'It's not for the faint-hearted,' says architect Tom Pike.

has been pushed back to provide space for a patio and allow the entire rear of the house to open up to the outside. It is an architectural act of high drama which has obliterated all sense of the dark and highly cellular house of 2004.

The brief was to bring light into the space and open up 'internal vistas', that is create views from one side of the house to the other. This is unusual in any house, and Victorian houses (with their strictly demarcated spaces – specific rooms for specific social and practical functions) are no exception. The design was worked up through a series of sketch proposals based on a careful study of the house and an acute understanding of the client's wishes, which were more aspirational than specific. In this house, internal walls were taken down and even the staircase, which remains in the same position, was replaced with a more permeable design in walnut. The balustrade marking the separation between ground-floor living room and the basement-level kitchen-diner is made of glass. Looking at the rear of the house from the back garden, it's a wonder the house manages to stand up.

'This did involve a lot of poured concrete and structural engineering with big chunky steel sections,' says Pike. 'It's not for the faint-hearted to undertake a job like this. But with the right engineer it's no problem. We really enjoy it.'

Contracturally, this was a very unusual job for The Pike Practice which, for 99 per cent of its projects, has a full contractural involvement up until the bitter end. Here, though, the client was extremely 'hands on' and highly energetic, and it was agreed that the architects would manage the scheme up until it received planning permission and building regulations approval, and then make themselves available as and when they were needed. Pike doesn't recommend this as a way of proceeding, but it worked here because both architect and client understood each other extremely well and spoke the same design language. 'The client is energetic, resourceful and has a good eye, so we could withdraw a little. He spent a lot of time on this house. I told him we were here whenever he needed us – and he did,' says Pike. The client even found the contractor (while the architect recommended the subcontractors)

above View towards the rear of the basement-level kitchen/diner. The garden was pushed back to create a patio.

left The glazed box at the rear of the house, covering the double-height space over the basement. The glazing is by specialist firm Cantifix.

who turned out to be rather good and relations remained positive throughout the build. 'We were called in to advise, and there was never a cross word or an argument. We would just say "that's not right, it needs to look like this" and the builder responded well. He had a particularly good understanding of the language we were using,' remembers Pike.

The client purchased the house for £760,000 and aimed to spend just £250,000 on this radical and comprehensive regeneration project. Pike cautioned that this was almost certainly insufficient and that the programme might well cost twice as much, but the client remained optimistic. Pike turned out to be right, and he suspects the client knew as much all along. For a building of this size, and with the finish and degree of intervention required for it, the client's original budget was hopeful, at best.

This house is a good example of what The Pike Practice does best. It's more than just rescue – it's tranformation through both a canny understanding of space and a keen attention to detail.

below left The fine finishes of this slick development are emphasised by the roughness of the concrete slab, positioned in front of the fire.

below, right Stair detail. This finely crafted structure is every bit as impressive as the glazed box at the rear of the house.

opposite The open-plan staircase replaces the Victorian original with a structure that permits more light to permeate through the house.

Kitchen extension for a terraced house, Islington, north London

SUMMARY OF WORKS	Extension for kitchen and courtyard garden
HOUSE DESCRIPTION	Victorian terrace
CONTRACT VALUE	£98,000
TIME PERIOD (planning through to completion)	25 months
RESULT	A house designed around the needs and personal style of the client; no need to move; no desire to sell
ARCHITECT	Plastik Architects

During what turned out to be a protracted and frustrating planning application process, there was a point when architect John Davies asked his client, 'Do you really want to do this?' She did, and the result is a kitchen extension of finesse and well-crafted intelligence.

The planning fiasco surrounding this extension project was out of all proportion to the scale of the works envisaged. The intention was merely to demolish a one-storey extension to the rear of a mid-Victorian terraced house and replace it with a structure that spread the full width of the house, filling in a narrow passageway, which ran alongside the old kitchen. Planning officials, however, refused permission on the grounds that Carolyn Wagstaff would be losing garden space. It was an irritating decision because the passageway (narrow and almost permanently in shadow) never formed part of the garden in any meaningful sense. Furthermore, argued the client, wasn't it up to her to determine just how much garden space she required? 'I couldn't believe that somebody was telling me what I could and couldn't have, when the only person it was affecting was me,' says Wagstaff.

The architects did two things: they appealed against the decision and revised the plan, shaving 1 metre (3.3 feet) off the proposal. This shorter scheme received the planners' assent, and when the appeals officer realised that the entire argument was over a single metre, he

opposite The flat-roofed, timber-clad extension contrasts with the Victorian brickwork of the terraces behind. A timber shutter screens views to and from the garden next door.

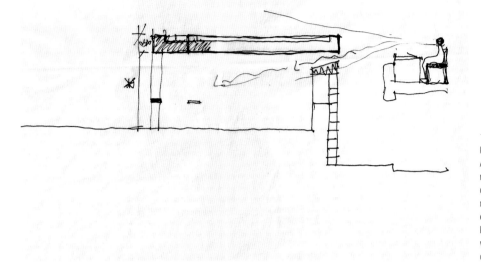

left Early sketch by Plastik
Architects showing the
relationship between the
original house (on the
right), and the proposed
extension (on the left).
Differences in floor heights
were one of the big
challenges on this project.

approved the original submission – leaving the client
with two approved schemes. Of course, she built the
bigger of the two, but the delay had cost her both time
and professional fees.

Wagstaff was introduced to Davies, a director of Plastik
Architects, after making an enquiry to the RIBA, which
supplied her with the names of four practices. An architect
friend also referred her to a fifth practice. These firms,
all young and small, were invited round to the house to
make an informal, off-the-cuff response to both the site
and a brief. This brief, written by Wagstaff after listing all
the things she liked and disliked about her original kitchen
space, was a statement of intent as well as a list of specifics
(see box). Importantly, it set the tone of the whole project,
'The extension should relate to the main house in a
metaphorical way (for example, light, airiness, materials) so
there is a relationship between the two; but it should not
be a pastiche of the Victorian house.'

Only Plastik could show a portfolio of built works;
Wagstaff even visited a home that the firm had worked on

to make sure the built reality matched the promise of the
photographs: 'It was just fabulous, and that absolutely
clinched it for me,' she says. Plastik got the job.

In building terms, the requirement was relatively simple
– to take out the narrow and rather mean kitchen at the
rear, while propping up the smaller bathroom above it
and incorporating a set of stairs down to basement level.
The job has been well executed from a narrow range of
building materials: concrete, timber, glass and painted
MDF. The floor is of very smooth, white concrete, which
required the attentions of a specialist subcontractor; the
kitchen worktop and the surface of the rear courtyard
garden have been cast from the same material. The
new rear wall is framed in oak with non-opening glass
windows and a cedar shutter that opens for ventilation.
It is an exercise in detail: everything is lined up and
angular. Even the thickness of the worktop is mirrored
in the thickness of the stainless-steel extractor fan,
while the stairway down to the basement has become
an unexpected little library with a view straight up to
the sky. It is a project of thoughtful and painstaking

above High-quality workmanship is a
defining feature of this project. Here, a
timber screen opens outwards, towards
the new courtyard garden beyond.

left The kitchen table was also designed by the architects for this position in the new kitchen.

below The kitchen extension ends with a courtyard garden of concrete. The clean lines of the interior continue outside.

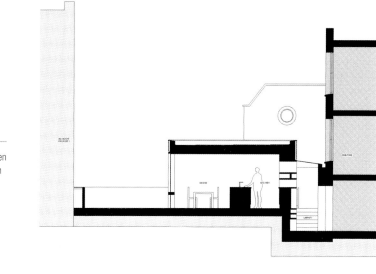

right Long section through the kitchen extension, showing the main house on the right and stairs, which negotiate different floor heights.

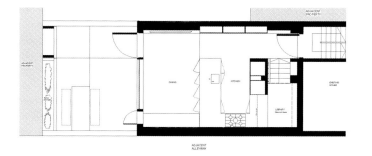

left Plan of the extension, with the courtyard garden to the left.

exactitude, driven by both the client and the architect: 'I had very high expectations, and John has exceeded them,' says Wagstaff. 'And I'm a perfectionist.'

But none of this was easy. Like many building projects, this one ran over time. Typically, the contractor produced work of high quality but the overall management of the job was less than effective, partly because the Polish contractor underestimated the time it would take. However, John Davies used a clause in the contract to penalise the builder for lateness – based on the rental value of the whole house, the builder would forfeit £600 for each week the project was delayed: 'It's a standard clause in the contract we recommended – the IFC 98 contract,' says Davies. 'This contract is often used for larger projects, but we think it best looks after clients'

interests in respect of matters such as late completion. The amount specified was our suggestion, which seemed fair on both parties.'

Davies had to make frequent site visits to ensure the design intention was not rushed through in a 'that'll do' manner, and a number of things had to be corrected after the architect's inspection, 'If it doesn't look right, then it isn't right,' he says. The job, finished in October 2007, was finished nine weeks late – meaning Wagstaff got £5,400 off the agreed price with the contractor. Thankfully, the builder didn't argue.

Even so, the project was not cheap. The cost of the build was roughly £98,000 and Davies' fee was 15% of that. There were also additional fees for other professionals

and the cost of unforeseen works, such as paying for a planning consultant, and rectifying cracks to the adjoining wall to appease neighbours. This works out at around £3,000 per square metre, which is a lot, but this project is not large and there is no room for economies of scale – if the building had been larger, it would not have cost much more. Wagstaff is adamant that the cost of this build has

given her a better quality space than she could ever have achieved by simply moving: 'I couldn't have upgraded as much for the budget. And anyway, I like it here.'

Furthermore, like other happy clients in this book, Wagstaff puts the success of the project down to the inventiveness and skill of the architect: 'Anyone doing a project like this would be crazy not to employ an architect. I wouldn't have had the vision and neither would a contractor. I think all this is amazing. People come in here and their jaws drop.'

The client's brief

The brief for the project is to construct a single-storey extension to the rear of the house to fill in the external space between the existing rear extension and the party wall, and to produce a new kitchen and dining area.

I'd like this extension to be an exciting and imaginative contemporary design, which creates a lighter and more spacious environment that transforms my home, and makes the garden an extension of the house like an outdoor room.

In our discussions other requirements that were highlighted were:
- The extension is to form an open-plan kitchen and dining area
- The kitchen units and fittings are to be replaced by new units and fittings
- The extension should relate to the main house in a metaphorical way (eg light, airiness, materials) so there is a relationship between the two but it should not be a pastiche of the Victorian house
- The extension should feel like a proper room not a conservatory
- It should be warm in winter and not hot in summer
- Views from the rear of the main house to the extension should be visually interesting
- The design should be clean in its detailing, ambitious in conception and provide a functional, liveable space

Here are a few likes:
- Under-floor heating
- Same or similar flooring in kitchen, dining area and garden
- Contrast of natural materials with modern finishes
- Plenty of storage space
- Floor to ceiling storage cupboards
- No wall cupboards above base units
- Island unit space permitting so I can face towards the centre of the room when preparing food
- Ease of cleaning and maintenance

I would like full architectural services, from design to completion of the construction works and for this service I understand you would charge approximately 15% of the total construction cost. The budget for the construction costs would be £70,000 which now includes £20,000 for the cost of a kitchen exclusive of VAT. This increases my total budget to £100,000 allowing for VAT on the construction costs but it would be good if VAT could be avoided.

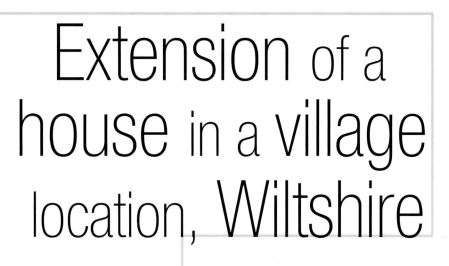

Extension of a house in a village location, Wiltshire

SUMMARY OF WORKS	Creation of a new living room; former living room becomes a central hall
HOUSE DESCRIPTION	Semi-detached cottage
CONTRACT VALUE	£77,000 (including floor and services)
TIME PERIOD (planning through to completion)	15 months
RESULT	Modernisation and expansion of a cramped house, providing more light and flexibility
ARCHITECT	David Thurlow Partnership

Architect David Thurlow says people in his profession should do two things: charge a proper fee and be 'absolutely up front' about everything that's going to happen on the project, which includes being 'open and honest' at all times. The result, he believes, is a system of transparency, which leaves room for few surprises and almost guarantees a confident client. This house, in the village of Monkton Farleigh, near Bath, is a good example of what can come from such an approach – such was the attention to detail with which this father–daughter team of architects managed the contract that the client actually paid less for their living-room extension than they had expected.

The house dates from the 1950s, although it looks older (it was built from the stone of a demolished barn). Tim and Annie Moss bought the house in 1997 and a conversation about extending this cosy cottage

opposite Unlike most domestic extensions, this development is at the front of the house, providing a new entrance and an entirely new approach to the original stone building.

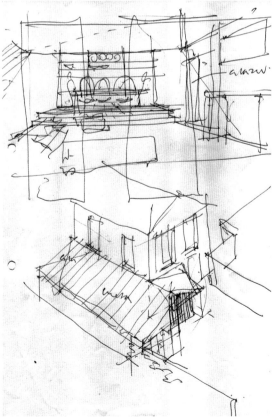

left Architect's early sketch, showing how an extension could wrap around the corner of the house (bottom). The top of the page indicates the dining area.

above Computer model of the scheme, created during the design phase of the project. The model is a close match to what was actually built; including the way the canopy is broken into shadow.

began around four years later. The clients were anxious to use a small local business and determined to build a contemporary structure within the setting of their distinctly picturesque village. The intention was to make visitors say 'wow!' Beyond that, there was no brief to speak of.

Suzanne Thurlow, the other half of the design practice, was living locally and was known to the client, so it was only natural that she should be asked for an opinion. But it was only after the client saw real examples of the practice's work that the appointment was made. The Thurlow 'design language' is loosely Modernist; contemporary and clean cut while being interlaced with an appreciation of a wide range of materials, textures and clever twists on traditional forms. A pair of tall triple-sash windows at the front of

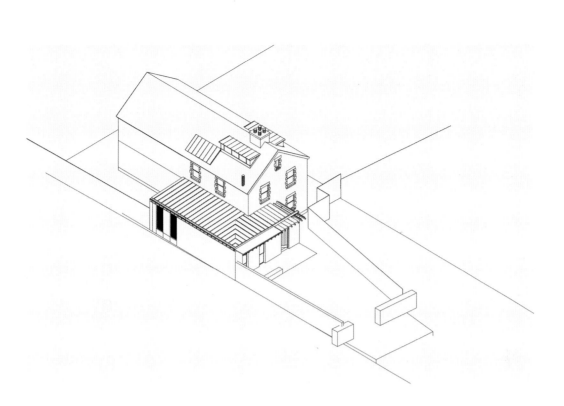

the extension are actually big enough to walk through: 'What look like sash windows are actually French doors,' says David Thurlow.

The extension wraps around the front and side of the house like an 'L', putting a living/dining room where there was once a driveway. The new structure also adds a generous front porch and what was once a snug living room (now moved to the middle of the house) is now a rather generous hall. From the outside, the new addition is clear to see – it is a rendered, flat-roofed structure nestled against a much more traditional building. Inside, however, the join is invisible.

In its completed state, the extension looks like a statement of common sense. Its location and the new system of circulation it generates (the front door was originally to the side, rather than at the front, as now) appear obvious. But the project didn't start out that way.

The design began as a series of sketches and suggestions; one involved a lot more glass and was bordering on a conservatory, which was rejected by the Mosses. This is all part of the process, though, and the Thurlows are committed to the idea that good architecture is a matter of testing a range of solutions until one's focus is narrowed down to a set of design moves that work on a variety of levels. It is a process of sketching (they carefully archive all sketches as evidence of the generation of an idea) and eliminating one option enables everyone to focus more fully on another. 'Even if the client doesn't like it, a proposal can give them something to react against,' says Suzanne Thurlow.

Once designs had been agreed and drawn up, they passed through the planning system unchallenged – helped, perhaps, because both client and architect attended the local parish meeting where the proposal was first considered (in a small community, it is harder to criticise a submission if the applicant is sitting in

left The glass and rough-sawn timber canopy at the front of the house. The extruded metal and weathered timber combine to form their own distinct architectural language.

opposite The front door opens onto a glazed porch. Finishes are fine, yet robust, and a bench doubles up as shoe storage.

the same room). Finding a builder proved trickier, the Thurlows approached three local builders and two came back with estimates. One would do the job, as specified, for £92,000, the other for £125,000. The architects revised their plans a little and then found a third builder who agreed a price of £68,000.

The Thurlows maintain there are two types of builder: the larger, more business-like firm that will very likely get the job done to budget and to time; smaller firms, however, might well put a higher premium on quality, will probably take more time, may well be a little less organised and will want to charge for 'extras'. The firm that undertook

the work on this project was one of the latter. The quality of the build is excellent, especially the joinery, but the biggest compromise was over the time the extension took to build. Although the programme was scheduled to last just 16 weeks, it actually took 42 weeks.

This phenomenal delay was purely down to the poor management of the contractor, which ended up having fundamental commercial problems and going out of business. Annie Moss, however, is philosophical about the process and the only real problem was not the mess but the lack of privacy: 'We had 10 people on site one day. It was the privacy issues that got to me,' she says.

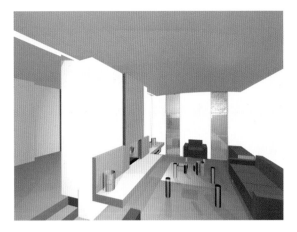

above Computer model of the
new living room, looking towards the
front. Even the fireplace has been
modelled.

below The hallway was
deliberately designed to
be large enough to double
up as another family room,
or study. Moreover, the
architecture is neutral
enough to accommodate
furniture from any era.

right The completed living room,
looking through into the new
hallway. The gentle curve of the
ceiling can be glimpsed.

above View from hallway through to the dining area, located up a set of steps. The dining area benefits from diffused light via glass blocks, preventing views directly onto a neighbour's garden.

Thankfully, the builder's contract had included a very precise list of materials, which the builder had to account for. This put the client in the curious position of having to pay out less to the contractor than they had planned, and the cost of the build came in at £1,709.95 less than anticipated.

Annie Moss is adamant that the best value for money was the flat fee of £10,000 for the Thurlow's architectural services: 'Without a shadow of a doubt that was money well spent, it really was,' she says.

What makes this extension so successful is that it works well during both day and night, summer and winter. It can open up as a light-filled, airy room and shut down as a snug box. Furthermore, the longer you look at this space, the sharper little details come into focus: the gentle curve of the ceiling, the built-in cupboards, the contrast between the fine carpentry of the beech doors and the deliberately rough-sawn timbers of the eaves. The planning permission included a loft conversion and it is only a matter of time before this family gets around to acting on that.

above, right The doors of the hallway are deliberately wide, allowing this central space to open right up to create a series of freely interconnecting rooms.

Living-room extension and house refit, Islington, north London

SUMMARY OF WORKS	Demolition of rear kitchen and replacement with new structure
HOUSE DESCRIPTION	Victorian terrace
CONTRACT VALUE	Undisclosed
TIME PERIOD (planning through to completion)	13 months
RESULT	A once shabby house has been completely reinvented and reorganised
ARCHITECT	Barbara Weiss Architects and Jones Associates Architects

This extension and remodelling of a mid-Victorian terrace was the result of an interesting architectural collaboration. One architectural practice took the project to planning, while another took over the job once permission was granted. This is relatively unusual, but it's a good example of the sort of profession that architecture is; although highly competitive, architects often know and trust each other, and will refer work to other practices if it's in everyone's best interest. In this case, the client approached Barbara Weiss Architects for no other reason than that they were nearby. Weiss, however, explained that her practice was relatively

opposite Rear view of the completed kitchen extension. Inside the garden/ courtyard, the construction material changes to timber.

expensive for domestic projects of this scale and advised that, once the broad design was settled, she would hand over the project to former employee Chris Jones for detailing and delivery. This system of referral worked well, and the clients have maintained good relationships with both firms of architects.

Built in the 1860s, the house had changed little since the 1970s, so when this couple of broadcast journalists bought it in 2005 it had become tired and shabby. The layout of the house was typical – a corridor flanked by a front room and rear dining room, which led to a single-storey extension containing the kitchen. The couple had moved from a flat where the kitchen had functioned as the heart of the home, so they wanted to recapture this style of living and take better advantage of the light and garden at the rear of the house. The design needed to

above The doors in the
closed position. At the time of
writing, the garden had not been
landscaped.

left The living space showing
both routes through to the front
of the house – through the
kitchen and the hallway, the
entrance of which is seen in the
centre of this picture.

be 'clean, 'unfussy' and 'contemporary without being
obsessively minimalist'. Other than that, the brief was
left relatively open.

Barbara Weiss developed a wide range of solutions, and
the client eventually settled on a design that located
the new kitchen in the centre of the house (in place
of the dining room). The dining room would shift to
the front, while a new extension at the back would
accommodate a living room running the full width of
the house. Additionally, a small first-floor bathroom,
which projected out over the old kitchen, would be
demolished and replaced with a space that ran the
length of the new living room below. This, however,
proved problematic because the neighbours feared the
first-floor extension would shade their own garden
and reduce the amount of light entering their rear
windows. This objection caused the local authority to
refuse planning permission. A 'right to light' expert
was drafted in (at a cost of £2,000), who scaled back
designs for the first-floor bathroom so that it projected
just 2.3 metres from the rear of the house, while
offering proof that this truncated version would not

opposite and right These images show the kitchen as a central connector between each end of the house, putting the kitchen literally at the heart of the building. This space is enlivened by a splash of colour, provided by orange glass.

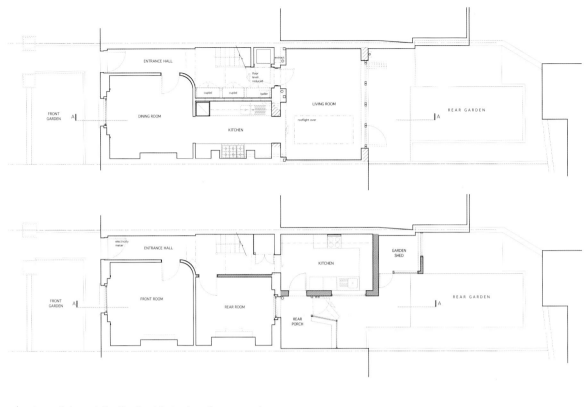

above Before and after. The plan at the top shows the new ground floor layout of this typical Victorian house. Walls shaded grey in the bottom drawing were demolished, including an internal wall, which was moved to widen the hallway and make space for cupboards. These plans were originally drawn at a scale of 1:50.

affect the neighbours' light. Planning permission was granted in May 2006, at which point the project was handed over to Jones Associates Architects.

It is important to understand that a building project is not fully detailed when planning consent is granted – permission broadly covers *what* is to be built (in terms of volume, mass, significant features and an indication of materials) rather than *how*. As well as managing the build, all the detailing in this project was designed by Jones.

Many, if not all the projects in this book are the product of good client–architect relationships built on trust and openness, and this is a theme that the owners of this house press especially hard. In particular, they stress that the relationship has to be well managed, respectful and

professional – if ideas are to be encouraged, they should not be quickly passed over by either the architect or the client: 'If you're not interested in exploring ideas that have never occurred to you, then you're not going to get very far,' says Jones.

Furthermore, once a way forward has been agreed, the architect needs to be allowed to get on with what he is trained to do. 'We have total faith in Chris's ability to do his job,' says one of the clients who is, anyway, too busy to get bogged down with what he is paying an architect to do, 'We have to let him do his work.' (Indeed, the professional manner in which this project was managed from the very beginning has meant that the client still has a good relationship with the neighbour, in spite of the right to light objection).

left This is a design aesthetic that welcomes contrast between old and new. Although original doors and mouldings have been retained, new design features and furniture are uncompromisingly contemporary.

Once Jones took over the project, structural configurations and design details needed to be settled (see box). Tests showed that the ground in the garden was too soft for standard foundations, so (after working closely with a structural engineer), a concrete 'raft' was laid on which the extension's steel frame could be erected. The extension does not rely on support from the house at all; it is its own independent structure. Jones also amended plans for a skylight in the roof over the new living-room as well as bringing space-saving tactics into the new (shortened) bathroom, such as incorporating the showerhead into a niche in the ceiling. Crucially, the client had the good sense to alert Jones to new requirements before it was too late, so the extra wiring for sound and lighting systems could

be incorporated at just the right stage. The completed project – constructed by a builder who Jones had worked with before, but who had just struck out on his own – has been skilfully executed. The choice of the builder appears to have been just right; prior to selection, the client visited a variety of Jones's projects to inspect the build quality of both expensive and cheaper contractors.

The clients moved out of their home for six months (having found the cheapest flat available) but the cost of renting still added around £6,000 to the price of the work. Jones's fee for his services was 14% of the build cost – normally it would have been 16%, but he agreed to a reduced rate because he had not taken the job through planning. Jones has, since the project's

above The hallway, shown here, was widened to allow the installation of cupboards, providing much needed storage in the house. This tactic narrowed the space that was to become the kitchen, but the trade-off works well for the client.

above View through from the new living space into the kitchen, which links the front and rear of the house. The skylight brings light flooding into the house.

completion, been retained by the client to undertake further work throughout the rest of the house, for which he will be paid by the hour; in fact, the 'phase 1' work involved putting the infrastructure in place for 'phase 2', including the correct positioning of electrical and plumbing elements.

Inevitably, this has been a disruptive process, but a frankly shabby house has been completely reinvented over the entire ground floor. 'It makes me smile every time I open the front door,' says the client. And although the extension is larger than the structure it replaces, the removal of an old aviary and other garden miscellany means there has been little or no loss of garden space.

above The first-floor bathroom. The showerhead is embedded in the ceiling, providing extra height for what is a small room with a low roofline.

right Again, the low ceiling in this bathroom is carved away to accommodate a skylight. With plenty of mirrored surfaces, this small space manages to feel much larger than it actually is.

Kitchen extension for a terraced house

Highbury, north London

SUMMARY OF WORKS	Replacement of rear extension
HOUSE DESCRIPTION	Victorian terrace
CONTRACT VALUE	£140,000 plus VAT
TIME PERIOD (planning through to completion)	2 years
RESULT	Larger, better-lit family spaces
ARCHITECT	Prewett Bizley Architects

Anna MacGillivray and Colin Butler always imagined employing an architect for a build project, but neither knew quite how to go about it or what to expect: 'It was a world that we didn't know about. We didn't know if an architect would want nothing to do with our little back extension or if it would cost us half a million pounds,' says Butler. So the couple went on a tour of architects' own homes during the annual Open House London weekend, when normally private buildings are opened up to the public for a limited period. During this time they visited architect Graham Bizley's house, then just recently completed, and filed his name away for future use.

opposite The timber extension to this typical Victorian terrace. The rear door has been set deep onto the structure, to provide a porch-like cover; this design tactic also modulates the design, preventing it from becoming a simple box.

Ideally, the couple would have bought some land and embarked on a new-build project, but because prices in London are so high they settled on purchasing an existing house and reinventing it. In June 2006 they paid £700,000 for a late-Victorian terrace that was not only 'tired and brown' but had no original features because it had been rebuilt after Second World War bomb damage. It was badly laid out – rooms were long, narrow and dark – and the main family bathroom was tacked on as a small, flat-roofed structure behind the kitchen (itself a long, thin space, like a 'train carriage', projecting from the main bulk of the house). This bathroom, cold and poorly located, also cut the house off from the garden: 'It was just what we were looking for,' says MacGillivray. 'We wanted a major project.'

left The windows open up
to create a large void in the
extension wall. This intelligent
extension was achieved without
planning permission – the work
was completed within permitted
development rights.

opposite Before and after.
The plan at the top shows the
original layout of the house;
the plan beneath illustrates the
house today.

MacGillivray and Butler approached Prewett Bizley Architects, then a relatively young practice, and were impressed by the enthusiasm and thoughtful approach that Graham Bizley and business partner Bob Prewett brought to their work. The architects also priced themselves cautiously (their fee was 12% of the build cost), and they were appointed in preference to another firm, which had also come to the clients' attention during those Open House visits.

What this client couple did not want was a straightforward box extension, for that they could simply approach a builder: 'We wanted a really good solution for the house,' says Butler, who now looks at his home and relishes the myriad of clever and thoughtful details that no building firm could provide on its own. 'Employing an architect just improves things on so many levels.'

First the architects prepared a study, for a fixed fee, containing three options ranging from, 'most floor space for smallest cost' to 'most interesting space for larger cost'. To the architects' surprise and delight, the client

opted for the latter solution. The proposal, which was developed via a number of variations, was essentially this: to demolish the two-storey rear wing of the house (containing kitchen, bathroom and bedroom above) and replace it with a structure that ran the full width of the building. The main bathroom would be relocated upstairs, allowing the new kitchen to open up to the garden. Furthermore (and this was the design element that really makes this little project interesting), the extension would include a little courtyard, cutting into the new space but bringing light and air directly into the middle of the house – in particular, the ground-floor dining room – where large glazed doors have replaced a small and insufficient window.

The design language is one of modern robustness: 'We really wanted to make the space interesting, as well as light and bright. This isn't a machined aesthetic,' says Prewett. The structure of the kitchen ceiling is clearly revealed, adding an element of texture to the room as well as providing niches to receive light fittings and increasing the head height slightly. The entire project

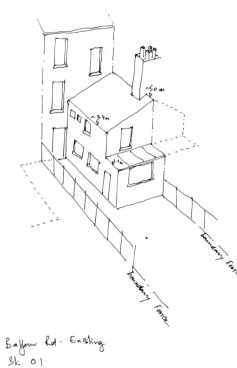

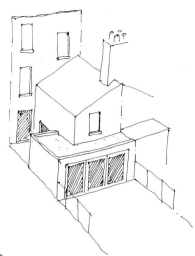

Balfour Rd - Existing
Sk 01

above Architect's sketch showing the original
condition of this terraced house, with a single-
storey bathroom extension at the rear (left), and the
altered building with the larger wrap-around kitchen
and central courtyard (right).

above The roof of this
extension is planted, a technique
that has not only insulative
properties but improves the views
from the upper floors. The small
courtyard space between the
extension and living room can be
seen at the bottom of the picture.

is, in some ways, a search for height; the windows
deliberately rise higher than the main structural
elements, overlapping with them slightly, and moving
the upper parts of the frames out of sight. Sustainability
is also important to the clients, and the architects have
responded well; apart from the structurally essential
steelwork at the back of the main house (hidden from
view), the extension is timber framed and clad in sweet
chestnut from approved sources. Even the kitchen
worktop is made from sheets of recycled plastic.

The whole project has been well executed, and clients
and architects are pleased with their selection of builder.
Choosing the right contractor was not merely a matter
of price, although that was the main consideration.
The clients visited builders on site to take a look at their
approach and quality thresholds. This also allowed them
to determine whether or not the builders actually wanted
to do the work. As it turned out, the contractor with the
best price happened to be the one they all liked the most.

The construction work did, however, take longer than
anticipated – mainly because the house required
some underpinning, which was unexpected: 'This

below The design process for this job evolved through a set of
slightly different options. Alternatives for window and door openings
were considered, as shown in these axonometric studies.

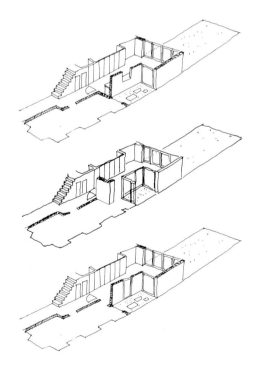

above, left The sill at the rear of the extension. It is wide and low enough to double up as a bench when the windows are open.

above, right The timber framing and boarding of this building project had been well executed. The sweet chestnut cladding was obtained from sustainable sources.

right During the design process the architects made a scale model of the proposal. This image shows the view from the living room through to the new extension. It bears a striking similarity to the built form.

opposite View to the rear of the extension, towards the garden. The window frames rise higher than the ceiling beams, adding to the impression of height.

above View towards the inner courtyard, with the corner doors in the closed position. The brick wall separating this property from the neighbours can be seen.

above View from the living room through to the rear. The opening to the inner courtyard replaces a small window; the doorway to the kitchen on the left is new.

is typical for existing dwellings,' says Prewett. 'Until you've taken the whole thing apart, you just don't know what you'll find. But at that point you can't turn back. You're committed. It's like a roller coaster.' Apart from pushing up costs, this turn of events delayed the project by around 10 weeks. The specialist subcontractor who supplied the bespoke doors and windows also added to the delay. Once made, the fitters arrived on site, tacked these elements into place temporarily and then disappeared – even leaving their tools behind. Bob Prewett was forced to find his own carpenter and finish the job himself.

This project is a good example of what can be achieved with both a good client and a thoughtful architect. Indeed, it is often said that clients get the buildings they deserve and that adage is certainly true in this case. Moreover, it is worth noting that this scheme was achieved without planning permission – all was achieved within permitted development rights (see glossary). The architects did request a Certificate of Lawfulness from the local authority. Although not strictly required, such a certificate does prove beyond doubt that an extension was built legally. In this case, obtaining the certificate was no faster than receiving planning permission. 'It does help when selling the property in the future,' says Prewett. 'It's professional good practice.'

Extension and refit of a house, Maida Vale, north-west London

SUMMARY OF WORKS	Kitchen extension, basement extension, interior fit out
HOUSE DESCRIPTION	Edwardian terrace
CONTRACT VALUE	£409,000 plus VAT
TIME PERIOD (planning through to completion)	20 months
RESULT	A thoroughly improved, modernised and extended family home, with space for live-in nanny
ARCHITECT	Katerina Hoey and HARTarchitecture

The wonderful remodelling of this Edwardian terrace in north-west London is an excellent example of how architecture can be used to extend, reimagine and refresh an elderly house, That is in spite of one or two minor snagging problems that pester even the most finely crafted of developments. Although the clients made efforts to do everything right (including commissioning the most expensive builder), the project went less than smoothly. Those builders, with a bit of help from recalcitrant neighbours, made the job more lengthy and painful than it need have been.

opposite The rear of the extension, with folding doors in the closed position. The external deck is laid at the same level as the internal floor. Garden storage cupboards are mirrored.

Ann Corbett and Martin Burke bought the house for £1.3 million in 2003. Notwithstanding a dangerously rickety conservatory, through which the family had to pass to access the garden, they decided to live in this house for a year before finally deciding how to improve the property. The house was full of promise – a basement offered the potential for an entirely new level of habitable floor space, while the replacement of the conservatory provided an opportunity to create a new family area opening up to the garden.

In 2004, having decided to embark on a construction project, the couple began looking for an architect: 'It was the first thing we did,' says Ann Corbett. They didn't conduct a formal search through the RIBA or the Architects Registration Board, instead, they asked friends and local people who'd had work done. Their enquiries took them to a local practice that rented office space to a sole practitioner, Katerina Hoey. 'We met and got on well. She was keen and enthusiastic,' remembers Corbett.

As it turned out, Hoey did not complete the job – her personal circumstances changed, she closed her office and passed the job on to architect Tracey Hart, who picked up where Hoey left off. This baton change worked well: 'Katerina and Tracey had exactly the same sense of style. They were exactly in tune. And everything they suggested, we tended to like,' says Corbett. 'We wanted contemporary, but not high fashion. Clean lines. No frills.'

above The rear extension, with folding doors in the open positions. The interior and the garden deck become a single space.

above View to the rear of the new extension, through to the garden beyond. Storage is slick and plentiful, and facilities are built in wherever possible.

above Elevation of the rear of the property. Flat-roofed and elegant, the extension makes a bold but polite mark in this Edwardian house.

The brief was relatively straightforward: to replace the conservatory, to construct a 'family kitchen', to add a dimension of flexibility to the house and to maintain, more or less, the footprint of the existing building. As discussions with the first architect progressed, it was decided to expand the basement by excavating to the rear of the house, providing sufficient space for a live-in nanny as well as a wine cellar, storage and a utility room. A planning application was submitted in November 2004, but it was withdrawn after planning officials (and a particularly awkward conservation officer), expressed concern about the size of the proposed extension, which was slightly bigger than the ageing conservatory it was replacing. The officials wanted a clearer delineation between the original house and the new structure, something that would make it appear less of an extension and more of an addition. Furthermore, one set of neighbours also needed persuading that the project would not adversely affect their views or right to light. The clients ended

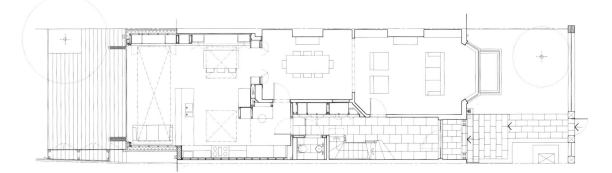

above Ground-floor plan of this development. The main entrance is shown bottom right. Skylights are indicated by dotted, diagonal lines

right Basement plan. Stairs are indicated bottom centre; the new light well, excavated at the front of the house, is shown on the right. A wine cellar is located bottom left.

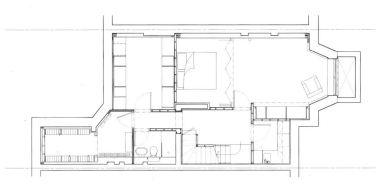

up employing a planning consultant to scrutinise the scheme; a revised plan was submitted in February 2005, and consent was granted.

By now, Tracey Hart had taken over the project and all detailed design, advice on the appointment of a builder and checking the works during construction was down to her. Building work was completed in two distinct phases. Phase 1, which cost £74,000 plus VAT,

below The generous kitchen area within the extension is enlivened by blue-backed glass splash backs. The kitchen units are from Siematic.

comprised excavating and damp proofing the expanded basement, including the creation of a basement-level light well at the front of the house; also, the conservatory was demolished and piling completed to make way for the rear extension. Phase 2 comprised all other building work, and this is where it gets interesting. Hart asked five builders to tender for the job, but only one replied, producing a figure of £330,000. This sum didn't sound unreasonable, but no one wanted to appoint a builder based on just one quote, so a further four builders were approached, all of whom replied. Quotes ranged from £300,000 to £343,000, so that original quote was not far off the mark. The decision was taken to appoint the most expensive contractor, after negotiating the price down to £335,000. Hart had worked with this firm before and knew them to be reliable and capable of high quality finishes (they have their own carpentry workshop). Also, they indicated they could start straight away. However: 'Overall, we are disappointed with everything,' says Ann Corbett. Hart agrees, and is frustrated that a firm that

she had worked so successfully with previously, could let themselves down so badly: 'I hate getting nasty, but I stopped saying please,' she says.

The builders did not start straight away, but five or six weeks after being appointed. Worse, the job overran by 13 weeks (the job eventually took 29 weeks, instead of the agreed 16). This was painful because the family (now with three children) moved into rented accommodation for the duration of the building work and, having given

above, left Kitchen diner, looking from the rear of the house. Skylights are equipped with blinds in case of glare.

above What makes this space so successful is its eclecticism. Here, Panton chairs (a modern furniture classic) surround an oak table. This is a place to be lived in, rather than a single, uncompromising design formula.

below and right Natural light is brought into the basement from a new glazed partition, which continues into the hallway above, flanking the staircase.

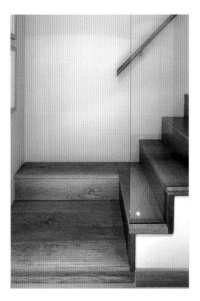

opposite, left The living room at the front of the house has also been entirely remade, with oak flooring and bespoke cabinets.

opposite, right As well as being extended, the entire house was refurbished, including this child's bedroom.

notice on their temporary home, had to move back into their house before work was completed. Much of the carpentry was of poor quality, promises were continually broken and the competence of the builders was marred by silly errors, for example, materials were not ordered in time. Hart had to force the contractor to redo jobs, and finally the client used a penalty clause in the contract to fine the builder for late completion.

Remarkably, even during the project's darkest moments, Corbett never began to regret embarking on the project: 'But we did regret certain things along the way, like using this particular contractor, although selecting them seemed like a good idea at the time.' Fortunately, Corbett had signed a full service contract with the architect, meaning that Hart was committed to overseeing the project to the bitter end: 'I always felt Tracey was there for us,' says Corbett.

In spite of the pain, and the odd bit of grouting that needs to be re-laid, the completed project looks effortless. The canny use of materials and well-placed glazing contrive to create a series of delightful spaces where texture, colour and light co-exist happily. The transition between original house and new extension is gentle, rather than stark, and the basement receives enough natural light to make it comfortable (helped not just by the newly excavated light well but by inserting a glass wall under the ground floor staircase, where the basement access is located). A bedroom/study has been decorated in anachronistic chocolate brown, but the result is seductive. Tracey Hart is clearly an accomplished interior designer and architect, capable of both the bold gesture and the light touch.

This project has seen the entire house refitted – there is not a square inch that has not been remade or altered in some way. To tackle such a vast job in one fell swoop is no mean feat, and probably more ambitious than the clients ever knew.

apartments
and basements

Basement kitchen for a terraced house, Canonbury, north London

SUMMARY OF WORKS	Replacement of basement kitchen
HOUSE DESCRIPTION	Grade II listed terraced house
CONTRACT VALUE	£115,000
TIME PERIOD (planning through to completion)	11 months
RESULT	A thoroughly modernised and enhanced space; prompted the remodelling of the rest of the house
ARCHITECT	Scape Architects

Chris Hartley's house in north London's Cannonbury tells two stories: on the outside it remains pretty much the 1820s terrace it has always been; on the inside, however, it is what Hartley calls 'a complete expression of modernity'. Hartley is the sort of client who is acutely aware that the lifespan of his house far outstrips his own, he resists any temptation to interfere with the Grade II listed building in a way that risks damaging its essential character.

'I feel a definite sense that I'm just passing through. This house was here for the best part of 200 years before I moved in and it will be here for many years after I leave,' he says. 'There is very little inside the house that is original and therefore worth preserving, but I do feel a sense of responsibility to preserve its outside appearance.'

Hartley bought the house in 1996 for £278,000. Its former occupant paid £210,000 for it in the 1980s and then spent a considerable sum refurbishing what had once been a very shabby and almost derelict place. The trouble was, as Hartley discovered, this extra investment had been a cosmetic makeover, rather than anything of substance, applied in a very slapdash manner. There had been little love expended on this house and Hartley gradually came to realise that, if the building was going to be anything more than a quick investment opportunity, it would have to become an architectural project.

opposite View towards the cooker. The timberwork is protected by a glass screen.

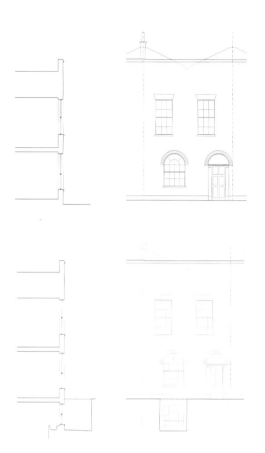

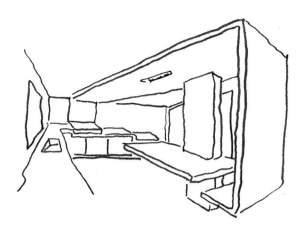

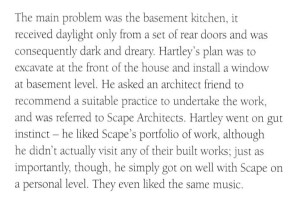

The main problem was the basement kitchen, it received daylight only from a set of rear doors and was consequently dark and dreary. Hartley's plan was to excavate at the front of the house and install a window at basement level. He asked an architect friend to recommend a suitable practice to undertake the work, and was referred to Scape Architects. Hartley went on gut instinct – he liked Scape's portfolio of work, although he didn't actually visit any of their built works; just as importantly, though, he simply got on well with Scape on a personal level. They even liked the same music.

'I always knew the relationship between me and the architect was going to be important. I wanted a personal recommendation and I was extremely lucky,' says Hartley. 'Scape seemed to me to be a bit cool, a bit edgy, keen to make a statement – clean lines and sweeping gestures. But they didn't come in with any preconceptions at all. They were very open-minded and listened to what I said.'

Originally, Hartley's basement contained two spaces, divided by a wall spanning the width of the house: a coal cellar to the front and a storeroom to the rear. At some point, the old coal cellar had become a corner room, which Hartley wanted to dispense with in order to open the basement right up (assisted by the addition of a window). Scape's natural inclination was to make the window opening fairly large and contemporary, but Hartley agreed with the conservation officer that it should be of similar proportions and style to the original windows above it. The conservation officer also pressed the case for retaining part of the wall to the coal cellar, as a sort of architectural 'memory'. This threw Scape's plans into a spin; dispensing with that wall had been one of the starting points for the whole project. Nonetheless, these suggestions were accepted and Scape's designs were redrawn accordingly. The large white column from which the central table cantilevers is a fragment of that original wall. Planning consent was granted, without challenge, during the summer of 2003.

left The basement kitchen, in plan, before being remodelled by Scape Architects. The stairs can be seen top left. There is no window at the front of the room.

left The basement kitchen, in plan, after building work. The kitchen runs the full width of the house and a window has been inserted at the front, requiring external excavation.

left Short section through the kitchen, showing the wrap-around timberwork and the cantilevered table. The new window can be seen in the background.

left Long section through the kitchen. The brown area indicates the timber panelling, which wraps around across the ceiling.

The finished project is a startling installation comprising elements of what could be called 'architectural furniture'. Ostensibly a kitchen, this space does successfully what all good kitchens should do, that is, double up as living and work spaces. The most eye-catching element, as the photographs show, is the strip of hardwood that wraps around the centre of the space to provide work surface, bench and ceiling. This joinery is complemented by more restrained surfaces of Corian (more worktops) and poured resin (the floor). The kitchen cabinets are constructed from cheap carcasses to which bespoke doors have been fitted. It is a well-executed job and one that seems to have delivered exactly what was promised in the architects' drawings. But, as ever, the translation from drawing to reality was not easy.

Hartley moved out for three months, which was the planned duration of the project; however, the work lasted six weeks beyond that. The problem encountered by Hartley and his architects was that the builders had an excuse for everything: 'You can never argue with builders. It's impossible,' says Hartley, who offers two pieces of advice for novice clients: 'find an architect you can work with' and 'be prepared for real pain with builders'. Hartley employed Scape to see the job through to the bitter end, so at least he had experienced professionals to fight his battles for him, but he still wishes he'd put more energy into selecting the main contractor. After Scape had put the contract out to tender, prices came in that seemed to bear little relation to the project: one firm of builders priced the job as high as another. Hartley and Scape didn't select the most expensive, but Hartley now wonders if he should have looked into the pricier options in case their quality thresholds were higher.

In truth, this piece of building work has been very well executed (both the kitchen and a new bathroom, off the basement stairs). It is a job that is a credit to both Hartley as client and Scape as architects. But that is not to say that the builders did not commit acts of crass stupidity. Once a specialist subcontractor had poured

above View from the rear of the kitchen towards the front. The timber element can be seen as a discreet piece of 'architectural furniture'. The resin floor had to be re-laid after being damaged by the builders.

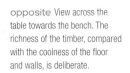

the resin floor, the main contractor had to perform some remedial work that involved welding – the floor was not covered for the duration of the work and the surface was damaged. A new surface has since been applied (paid for by the builder) but Hartley is irked because the colour and texture is not as good as the original. Hartley's frustration is understandable, however, architecture is not product design and the risk that the finished project will be marked by foolishness or inattention to detail, even in the smallest way, is always high. Building projects are invariably one-offs, and can be considered almost as well-made prototypes.

Since completing the project in May 2004, Hartley invited Scape back a year later to remodel the rest of the house in the same spirit as the basement – a project that has now been completed.

Apartment refit, Chelsea, west London

SUMMARY OF WORKS	Complete internal refit
HOUSE DESCRIPTION	Apartment in mansion block
CONTRACT VALUE	Undisclosed
TIME PERIOD (planning through to completion)	2 years
RESULT	Radically remodelled interior much improved light, finishes and services
ARCHITECT	Platform

Platform Design Group is not a standard residential design practice. Rather, this firm is a collection of interior and graphic designers with expertise in retail, exhibition and commercial spaces – they've even designed a Yo! Sushi restaurant and a training centre for Virgin Atlantic. None of this makes the firm the obvious choice for reinventing this late 19th century, two-bedroom apartment, but this was a job with a difference. The Russian clients were looking for such a high level of quality (indeed, perfection) that the project could be treated almost as the fit out of an aircraft, or a luxury yacht. Platform was commissioned for its knowledge of materials, fanatical obsession for precise detailing and experience in handling expensive appliances.

When Max Eaglen, director of Platform, first saw the flat it was 'tired and dreary', with stripy wallpaper and a poor quality, faux cottage kitchen. Being more than a century old, walls were out of alignment, 90-degree corners and flat surfaces were non-existent. Moreover,

opposite The kitchen, supplied by Minotti. The care with which these units were made had to be matched by careful installation.

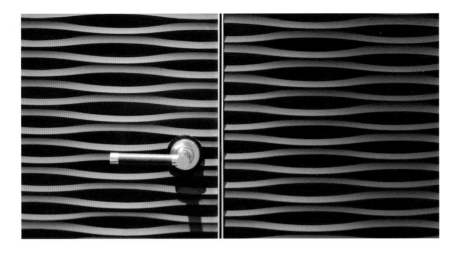

opposite View down the hallway towards the leather-clad wall. A fireproof strip of glazing has been inserted into the wall on the left, bringing light in from the living room.

left Detail of the hallway wall. The surface is highly textured from a cladding of timber strips, which have been sprayed to give them a suede effect.

the client (a family of three), had set their hearts on kitchen and bathroom appliances, which were too large for the spaces available: 'We quickly realised walls had to come down,' says Eaglen. This gave the designers the opportunity to inspect the structure of the apartment itself and remedy weaknesses that would otherwise have gone unnoticed. Building new walls also allowed them to construct surfaces that were strong enough on which to hang limestone tiles – which would have proven too heavy for the original partitions.

Before proceeding with construction work, the client needed to secure the permission of the freeholder, which was granted with no objections although merely waiting for a reply delayed things a little. Time was clawed back by making a building regulations application to a specialist consultancy, rather than direct to the local authority. As the building isn't listed and no external works were planned, planning permission was not required. The design phase proceeded in close consultation with the client. This was not the sort of job where the designer listens to a brief, only to go away and return with plans. Here, the family followed the design team every step of the way, each with their own specific interests. One was particularly anxious about the way the living room would accommodate his large furniture; another, who Eaglen says has a particularly discerning eye, was most concerned with finishes and soft furnishings; and another's interest lay with the kitchen. The dogged attentions of these three had to be considered within a single design, which wouldn't

have been difficult to achieve if the spaces within this apartment had not been so small. Clever and subtle shoehorning was paramount.

The bathroom is a good example of how the designers have responded to this demanding brief. The clients wanted (among other fine items including a sink carved from solid limestone) a Dornbracht shower, which recreates the effect of a shower of rain. This meant installing a separate water tank to feed it. Astonishingly, Platform has managed to make this small bathroom actually feel a little roomy: 'There's so much going on in here, but you'd never know. It was a real exercise in planning,' says Eaglen.

There are further surprises. One wall running the length of the hallway is clad in a mesh of timber slats (from American firm Mobilia) that has been sprayed with a product often used in the airline business to create a suede effect. At the end of the corridor is a door and wall covered in leather: 'It's absolutely beautiful and immaculately finished. We wanted to warm things up a bit,' says Eaglen. Even the frameless glass door, which leads to the living room, was an exercise in exactness – if it was to have fireproofing qualities a perfect fit was essential. The frame was manufactured and installed on site, and then demounted and shipped to Austria where a glazing specialist manufactured a door to match. 'This isn't cheap,' adds Eaglen.

opposite The bathroom. The sink is carved from a single piece of limestone, while the porthole window disguises a shabby sash-window behind the partition.

right The Dornbracht rain shower. This unit requires so much water that a special tank had to be installed.

The installation of the Minotti kitchen was also handled with immense care. The units were finished by hand and are therefore unique, so the installation could not be the rugged and robust activity that tends to characterise these things. Subcontractors were carefully managed to ensure that as few people as possible were on site during the installation, reducing the chances of accidents and lapses of attention. Plumbers, electricians and tilers were carefully choreographed to ensure the kitchen units remained pristine. 'We literally locked the door on the kitchen during installation to stop anyone from carelessly walking in,' remembers Eaglen. The perfectionism is almost boundless. When the limestone bathroom sink was delivered, Eaglen found that the water didn't drain as well as intended, so the bowl was reground on site: 'We just wanted everything to be perfect,' Eaglen says. Thankfully, it is, and the client has now set the design practice to work on a house outside London.

Apartment refit, Battersea, south London

SUMMARY OF WORKS	Refit of apartment
HOUSE DESCRIPTION	Duplex penthouse, built 1999
CONTRACT VALUE	£350,000
TIME PERIOD (planning through to completion)	25 months
RESULT	An interior that properly matches the building and its prominent location
ARCHITECT	Form Design Architecture

The interior of this large penthouse atop a 1999 development overlooking the Thames bore little relation to the building itself. The apartment block, designed by architectural firm Aukett, is broadly of a contemporary design and very much of its time but the interior fit out was clearly masterminded by someone with very different ideas. The three-bedroom apartment, overlooking Battersea Park and giving glimpses of the Albert Bridge, was an exercise in middle-of-the-road blandness; what appeared to be a slick and alluring duplex from the outside was, in fact, replete with the coving, pointless flourishes and pelmets of ordinary suburbia. The work wasn't carried out particularly well and the general space planning left much to be desired. 'It was a very poor and traditional fit out,' remembers architect Malcolm Crayton of Form Design Architecture. 'It was as if the developer panicked.'

Crayton began talking to the client after being referred by a mutual friend. The management consultant had already lived in the apartment for a couple of years and, at first, asked the architects to help simplify the fussy décor and add a dimension of coherence to his home. From the living room, for example, the view to the Albert Bridge was obscured by the kitchen, removing one of the reasons for buying the property in the first place. Walking through to the generous balcony required stepping over the sliding mechanism of the glass doors, a visually intrusive installation flaw as well as a trip hazard.

The client–architect conversation began slowly, and gradually a more complex and ambitious brief began to evolve. More importantly, both parties got on very well and trust was established very early on. Everybody considered the job as a series of problems to be solved – there were few preconceptions: 'This couldn't have happened without a sympathetic architect–client relationship,' says Crayton.

What began as an exploration into joinery solutions (a series of discreet jobs to be completed by a well-

directed carpenter) eventually became something far more ambitious. The key design move involved cutting through the concrete slab that formed the ceiling of the living room and the floor of a bedroom above. This would have created a generous double-height space, which would have opened up views of the sky from deep within the living room; also, the balcony created from the former bedroom would have made the apartment a less compartmentalised place.

Unfortunately, this idea was never allowed to materialise due to a complaint from the immediate neighbour. Because of the way the freehold agreement for the building was drawn up, just a single objection is enough to prevent building works inside any apartment. The objection was purely on the grounds of the noise that the neighbour imagined he would have to put up with. No amount of talking could resolve the issue, and the refurbishment project was delayed for a year.

Without the double-height space, the architects were forced to work even harder to create the kind of spaces that would do justice to a property in this location. The wall between the living room and kitchen was taken out and a sliding one put in its place, making oblique views to the river possible and bringing more light inside the building. The principal social space was

divided into three zones – living, dining and watching TV – the furniture for these spaces was plotted very precisely. Almost everything was remade. The stairs were enclosed and made to feel more solid with French limestone cladding; walls and storage spaces were installed in a more integrated manner (cupboards and air conditioning services are part of a coherent whole rather than added on); floors were re-laid in timber and stone, after installing enough acoustic insulation to prevent sound from travelling down to the apartment below; most of the joinery was either replaced or simplified. Now, the sill of those sliding doors is buried within the depth of the floor.

The budget and energies of the architects were often focused on the areas which really needed it, so the apartment still contains vestiges of its original fit out. This was not a wholesale demolition and rebuild project, but rather one of casting a critical eye over what would be allowed to stay and what should come out. Some of the original skirting board remains, for example, though stripped of unnecessary mouldings: 'We tried to make sense of the materials, and just calm it all down,' says Crayton.

This approach provided a handful of opportunities for genuine indulgence. Form eventually made a virtue of the neighbour's complaint. The bedroom that was to become smaller by having some its floor removed is now the master bedroom complete with a beautifully crafted teak bath set behind a screen of timber slats.

This space, arguably the most delightful space within this transformed home, owes something to the feel of a boutique hotel – the bath is in a zone of its own, raised on a platform (containing the water services) which is accented by 'green tea' marble plaster.

Crayton says: 'Form views architecture as the art of theatre rather than fashion. The idea is to create spaces that are animated by the lives of people. 'Our architecture is not about noise. It's about being pragmatic and responsive, appropriate and discreet. People can then use their spaces in any way they want to.' This project is a success because the client has not been given a set of spaces that are pompous expressions of an architectural conceit; they are spaces for living in. Indeed, the client continues to invest in the apartment and suggests tweaks and minor changes here and there, but he always calls the architect first. As the original brief evolved, so does the property.

opposite Colour and texture: the teak and 'green tea' plaster provide a warmth to this clean, contemporary design. Modern architecture need not always be about white, featureless surfaces.

Creation of an apartment on a warehouse roof, Shoreditch, east London

SUMMARY OF WORKS	Rooftop extension
HOUSE DESCRIPTION	Two-storey apartment
CONTRACT VALUE	Undisclosed
TIME PERIOD (planning through to completion)	5 years
RESULT	A generously proportioned family home in an unexpected location
ARCHITECT	Tonkin Liu, with Richard Rogers

This eye-catching rooftop development in east London's Shoreditch does not quite fall into the same category as the other houses in this book. It is not an elderly house remade, rather, it is a new dwelling placed on top of a pre-existing structure. This two-storey, six bedroom duplex makes first class use of space that would otherwise have gone unnoticed, adding value where you would least expect it.

For all its clean-cut Modernist elegance, this home is a place for all the senses, including touch. The fluorescent front door is everything a front door should be: thick, wide and heavy in an almost medieval sense. The

opposite Two-storey addition to warehouse building by architects Tonkin Liu, in London's Shoreditch

sliding screen, which divides the kitchen and main living space from the master bedroom, is so robust and massive it is surely bombproof. Yes, the apartment has a computerised building management system, but the architects (and their client who wishes to remain anonymous) are to be applauded for not motorising that screen. In an age of flick-of-the-switch convenience where anything can become mass-less, it is nice to put your back into something.

Tonkin Liu Architects worked on this project over a period of five years. The development is structurally complex, but that is nothing compared with the legal wrangling that almost brought the whole thing juddering to a halt on a number of occasions. 'I think it died three times, but each time it came back to life. Each time there was a different stumbling block. For us it was no ordinary architectural journey,' remembers Mike Tonkin.

There is not room here to rehearse in detail the ebbs and flows of this project's genesis although they are easily imagined when one considers the following: access to the apartment is courtesy of a lift in the newer building next door as well as a bridge, which occupies 1 square metre (10.8 square feet) of a neighbour's balcony. In fact, it even came as a surprise to the owner of the building's roof that the air rights (ie the space above the surface of the roof) were owned by someone else. For a number of years this project was characterised by the constant round of negotiations and never-ending fees rather than by architectural invention: 'At one point there were seven legal teams working on it,' says Tonkin. Legal negotiations were completed in the summer of 2005.

Quite apart from the matter of 'air rights', the roof of this former warehouse offered further problems. Second World War bomb damage to the centre of the building had been repaired by using columns, which were less robust than those they replaced, so the building's perimeter is stronger than its heart. This meant that the architects had to spread the load of the apartment out to its edges; there are no internal columns and the apartment literally hangs from a frame that is set atop the building. The frame (which was assembled in just seven days), doubles up as a shading device, around which wisteria and clematis now creep, providing further summer shading and withering away when winter light is needed.

It is a thoughtful little building this, in the sense that much thought has been expended on it. There's almost nothing in the apartment about which Mike Tonkin cannot wax lyrical: the four kids' bedrooms, lined up like monks' cells; the shower head, set so high above the bath that the water feels like tropical rain; the cheap prison mesh (knitted so finely it can't be climbed) lining the balconies and balustrade; the care with which spaces, and external views are framed: 'It's all about relationships and proportions. Proportion costs you nothing, but it makes a huge difference,' says Tonkin.

below, left West elevation of the former warehouse, where a new two-storey apartment now sits. The original building was strong and robust enough to sustain this large addition.

below, right South elevation of the development. The spiral stair up to the rooftop garden can be seen on the upper right.

opposite Planting is an important part of the overall vision for the development. As well as providing additional shading in the summer months, the fragrance of wisteria and clematis are drawn into the apartment through the under-floor ventilation system.

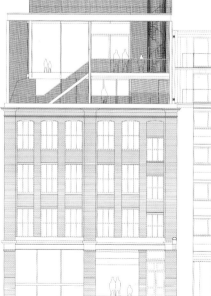

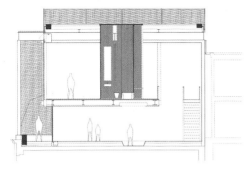

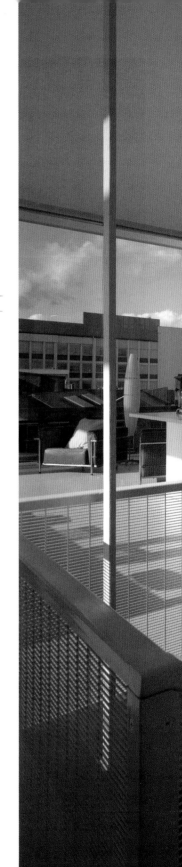

left Section through the apartment, showing the extremely high bathroom in the centre. The 'conversation pit' can be seen on the lower floor.

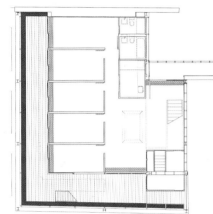

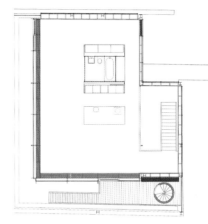

above Plan of the lower floor. The entrance is found on the top right; bedrooms are ranged along the left. A terrace wraps around two sides of the development (seen on the left and bottom of the drawing).

above Plan of the upper floor. The kitchen island is indicated by the rectangle in the centre, while the bathroom unit can be seen as a square in the upper portion of the drawing. A large sliding door (stored in a slot behind the kitchen cupboards) can be pulled out from this unit, towards the wall on the left, to create a bedroom space that is separate from the living room/kitchen in the lower part of the image.

So what's it like to live here, in this showcase of ideas? Actually, it's every inch the family home, although many standard domestic features are lent something of a twist. Within the hall the floor drops into a 'conversation pit'; it is from here that you watch television, beamed onto a wall from a ceiling mounted projector. Apart from the lurid front door, colour is added by the furniture, the planting and all the accoutrements of family life (stickers have been cheekily applied to the steelwork). In fact, during the design phase, Tonkin Liu and the client wrote extensive lists of all the things that would add colour to the whites and greys of the space itself.

opposite View looking down towards the entrance, picked out in fluorescent paint. Applied colour is unusual in this development. The occupants themselves – along with furniture, books, food and other accoutrements of living – were imagined as adding colour.

The space planning is also slightly curious. The four children's bedrooms (plus guest room) are located on the lower floor, off the grand hallway, while all other spaces – the living and dining areas, parents' room and family bathroom – are found in the double-height vastness of the upstairs where the views are better. The very open-plan nature of this upper space is made possible by clustering a wide range of facilities into a central pod, set off-centre. This pod provides everything from kitchen cupboards (on one side), wardrobes (on

the other), the bathroom, a small desk area, a central switching system and the docking mechanism for that large sliding door, which cuts the space in two at bedtime. Almost everything is integrated. You would have to look very hard to find an afterthought.

None of this is meant to imply that this crisply detailed home is wall-to-wall luxury. It isn't. Money has been spent where necessary; the glazing is almost as big as it gets, while the Corian kitchen worktop must have been far from

cheap. Money has also been saved where appropriate; there are wardrobe doors from IKEA, plain lino covers the floor and polycarbonate lines the walls of the bathroom.

This project could not have been achieved without the support of an enlightened and architecturally astute client. For a client with more conservative tastes this could easily have become a place of gadgets and expensive finishes, which is hardly the point of this house.

above The apartment has been configured to make the most of London's changing skyline. Since this image was taken, Foster + Partner's Swiss Re building has become obscured by other buildings.

primer chapters

How to find the

Any homeowner, having taken the decision to extend, remodel, amend or refurbish their house, needs to ask themselves one key question: do they actually need an architect? This book is an exploration of the ways that homeowners have 'invested in design' by employing an architect or other trained designer to help rethink their house; but it's worth bearing in mind that many jobs don't necessarily require the attentions of a design specialist. A simple conservative extension, similar to the one next door, could well be built by a competent builder with no architectural advice at all. The same applies to garage-into-study conversions. Loft conversions too can be left in the hands of specialist contractors. It just depends on how visionary you are. Do you want just a few more square feet, or something better?

Of course, it is always worth asking for an architectural opinion and someone (keen to build up their portfolio or experiencing a lull between larger jobs), might be happy to take your job on. Equally, the architect may see some hidden potential in your otherwise workaday project, so it would be unwise to dismiss the idea of an architect out of hand.

At the time of writing there are approximately 30,000 registered architects practicing in the UK, and the number of students signing up to architecture courses appears to be increasing annually, so there is no shortage of expertise and architects are relatively easy to find. The trick, however, is finding the right one. Word of

mouth is still a reliable way of finding an architect – it is not merely the architect's designs that the client is buying, it is also the architect's personal style, work ethic, value system, contacts and experience. A personal recommendation should be able to address all these issues. Web searches are, obviously, an effective way of drawing up a list of architects in your area, but perhaps a more reliable way of obtaining a list of relevant specialists is to contact your local branch of the Royal Institute of British Architects (RIBA) or the equivalent body in Scotland, Wales and Northern Ireland (see the directory later in this book). Elsewhere around the world other national institutes play a similar role in maintaining professional standards and promoting the work of their members, such as the American Institute of Architects, the Royal Australian Institute of Architects and the Singapore Institute of Architects.

The RIBA represents around two-thirds of practising architects and its central Client Services unit in London can provide recommendations, while its 12 regional offices will probably be able to draw up a list of names

opposite **Alastair Howe Architects, Extension and Improved Layout to a 1960s House, Berkshire.** The new front door of an extended house in Wokingham, Berkshire. The client drew up a short list of architects after consulting with the RIBA and reading books.

right architect
for your project

that is more tailored to your needs. Since the mid-1990s the RIBA has also run the 'Architect in the House' scheme every summer, which pairs homeowners with local architects in return for a minimum donation of £40 to the homeless charity Shelter. These consultations are a good opportunity for people to meet architects for a quick no-obligations chat.

Membership of the RIBA is not obligatory, so if you find an architect who does not put the august institutional logo on their business card that is certainly not a cause for worry. In fact, many architects are RIBA members for the simple reason they can use the logo. Membership of the Architects' Registration Board (ARB) is compulsory, and anyone practising as an architect without an ARB registration number is acting illegally. Checking on the registration of your architect is simple – just call the ARB (or visit its website www.arb.org.uk).

Another, more creative, way of finding an architect is to leaf through property and design publications, making a list of names and projects as you go. Being featured in a glossy magazine is not a sign that an architect is too big and successful for your project (conversely, a lack of public exposure is not a sign of a lack of competence). The benefit of publicity to architects is that it could well generate new business, so they will welcome a call that has been prompted by an article in a colour supplement. And even if a literature survey does not lead to a direct appointment, it can at least provide a wealth of inspirational designs from which to formulate your own brief. Magazines and web searches are also good sources of award winners – the architectural community is awash with annual prizes, covering everything from conservation and the work of young practices to the best use of brick, and building of the year (the RIBA Stirling Prize, announced every October, is the one

opposite **Adam Dennes, CaSA Architects, Extension and Rescue of a Village House, Hampshire.** The client of this extension, used the services of a family friend. The architect was relatively young and inexperienced, but the level of trust was high.

to look out for). It is unlikely, although possible, that you will approach the Stirling Prize winner to redesign your house, but it is certainly worth looking at the regional short lists to get a view of what contemporary architecture is all about at a local level. No architect will want to be told to design in the style of another architect, but to be able to provide some names and images, just as a starting point, will enable a designer to get a feel for what you're after.

Architects will also recommend other architects. The world of architecture is very small – design practices keep a very close eye on each other and the profession is characterised by a friendly rivalry. Very often staff will leave a practice to set up in business on their own, and this is generally done with no malice and often with the positive support of the original employer. In fact, some practices are actually proud of the number of spin-off businesses they have generated. Furthermore, architects can be serial networkers and may well teach at universities where they rub shoulders with their peers and form professional relationships with students. The result of this intimacy is that if you approach an architect who is, for whatever reason, unable to make room for your job, it is very likely he or she will be able to recommend someone who can take you on. Even large practices, too busy for domestic work, will be able to refer you elsewhere, especially if they are one of those businesses that have provided the breeding ground for other practices. There are even occasions where practices take a job through to the planning stage and then hand it over to a competent but less expensive firm to get it built.

Architects train for many years in a highly regulated environment, passing through 'Parts' 1, 2 and 3 before they can legally call themselves professionally qualified. Architects should be reasonably competent (and many are highly effective) once they have completed Part 2 (a post-graduate course of study that they undertake at architecture school after their first degree) but officially, they are unable to call themselves architects. In fact, some design firms produce superb work without first having gone to the trouble of qualifying to Part 3 level (which incorporates a period of recorded work in a practice and professional exams). But while all this training is designed to raise building designers to

a certain level of expertise, its completion does not mean that any fully-qualified, ARB registered architect is right for you. Before appointing any architect you need to arrange an interview – not to ensure they are up to the job (they probably are) but to make sure you can actually work together and remain in a positive relationship for the duration of the project. You need to ensure that each of you, client and architect, have a similar understanding of the scope and goals of the project, that you share the same agenda and can reach an agreement over budgets. Some architects might, for example, have a tendency to reinterpret the brief and go off on a wild tangent, while others may have a particular interest in, say, recyclable building materials, conservation or Modernity. You need to understand each other and be clear about what you are each trying to achieve – without this, the result will inevitably be frustration.

You will also want to see examples of the architect's work (photographs as well as drawings) to establish their track record in the type of work you have in mind. This is not necessarily a matter of seeing how many extensions or conversions they've done; you also need to establish: if they can work within your budget, if they can work on the scale of your project, and if they can face up to the specific challenges of your property (including planning or conservation issues, access difficulties or the peculiarities of the local geology). Ask for references from previous clients and, if appropriate, visit completed projects. And remember that it isn't just the quality of the finished building that matters – it is how well it measured up to the brief.

Remember also that during the selection process, the architect is also interviewing you. Your choice of architect will have a crucial effect on the outcome of the project, and it is equally true that clients get the projects

left **Alastair Howe Architects, Extension and Improved Layout to a 1960s House, Berkshire.** The owners of this 1960s house originally considered demolition and replacement. Architect Alastair Howe, who drew this sketch, liked the house and warned the client that if they wanted it replaced with something more conventional then he was the wrong architect.

they deserve. Architects will shy away from clients who don't appear to know their own mind and lack the ability to make a decision; conversely, clients who know only too well what they want (and aim to engage an architect merely to 'draw up' their own naive scheme) will also sound warning bells. The aim is to find an architect with whom you can build a relationship, as well as a house; and that relationship needs to be founded on honesty, plain speaking and a firm commitment to the underlying principles of the project. 'The most important thing,' says Wiltshire-based architect Nigel Bedford, 'is that everybody is absolutely clear and up-front about what they want to do, when they want to do it, and what the risks are.'

Being a good client is as much of an art as being a good architect (there are awards for clients, too). The role of client is one of being a patron rather than a tyrant. Yes, you are paying the bills and, yes, you get to live in the house when the job is done – but that does not provide a licence for constant changes of mind, a deluge of emails to which you expect rapid responses, and the withholding of fees. If, after an interview of two to three hours, you make your selection carefully and you consistently behave in the manner of an enlightened (though determined) individual, that will count as much as well-honed design skills.

Writing a brief

Part 1 – The Brief

Good design is all about process. It evolves, powered by the spirit of genuine enquiry and the exploration of ideas. Nothing is obvious and those pieces of architecture that look almost effortless are very probably the result of much mental agony. Do not expect an architect to answer your brief instantly with a single, fully worked out solution.

The better the brief, the better the solution. In fact briefs demand a considerable amount of effort, so are best worked through with your architect, not imposed on them as a set of independently composed rules. Of course, the brief will very likely include some core, non-negotiable ingredients that catalysed the whole design process in the first place, such as 'extra bedroom', 'more living space' or 'better library'. These demands are essential to describe the parameters of the project; they identify, at the most fundamental level possible, the what, but not the how. Then there are a myriad other considerations: the question of light, materials, style, budget, timescale etc. These are things that could well benefit from discussion with your architect, rather than being worked out in advance. You will also need to consider how you will use these new spaces: will they be public, family-orientated places or very private ones? Do you want to capture or screen out a particular view? Do you want to weave a new structure subtly into the fabric of an elderly structure, or counterpoint it with something distinctly contemporary? A general sense of

the answers to these questions will affect the selection of your architect, but it would probably be a waste of time to dwell on them in too much detail. Apart from anything else, you are appointing an architect as a generator of ideas, and an extra set of eyes to see what you can't see, so second guessing them or trying to pin them down too early is a recipe for the missed opportunity.

Neither should you try thinking like an architect, adopting architectural idiom and conceit. It is not uncommon for clients to artificially curtail the scope of their project because of, say, imagined foundation problems and structural questions. Similarly, a client might also encumber an otherwise sound aspiration with unnecessary and erroneous detail. It is perfectly reasonable for a client to imagine, for example, that a structure of cheap softwood is unsuitable for a wet climate and specify a building of masonry – but timber, in wetter countries than the UK, can be a reliable and long-lasting building material if detailed and maintained well. Try not to anticipate the views of the architect; stick to your vision and the details will resolve

opposite **David Thurlow Partnership, Extension of a House in a Village Location, Wiltshire.** The architects were so precise with the scheduling and pricing of construction elements for this project, that the builder could not go over budget. The build actually cost less than envisaged.

and employing an architect

themselves at the appropriate time. All building projects orientate themselves around the three issues of time, money and quality. Part of the process, which generates the brief, will be to examine the relative importance of each of these elements.

Once you have found your architect, or during the selection interview, you need to discuss the terms of appointment and fees (discussed in more detail later in Part 2). The architect will then set down in a Letter of Agreement the broad scope of the job and the terms that apply. This letter, which needs to be signed by both parties, might run to four or five pages and be very contractual in tone, including details of the architect's insurance cover and dispute resolution procedures. One of the key questions to be settled at this stage is at what point you would like the architect to conclude their work. It is not uncommon for architects to disengage from the job once planning permission has been achieved (after which the drawings are handed over to the client for their builder to interpret); alternatively, the architect might be required to stay with the project and secure Building Regulations permissions. They may, however, provide the full service, which means sticking with the project until the bitter end, sourcing the surveyors and contractors, project managing the work and signing the building off once the builders have departed.

This 'full service contract' will obviously be more expensive than commissioning an architect for just one part of the job, but it is a more reliable way of translating the vision into reality. Deciding when the relationship with your architect will end is one that should not be taken lightly. Architects insist (of course they would) that employing them right through to sign-off will be reflected in the final value of the project. They have a point – drawings can always be the subject of misinterpretation (accidentally or otherwise), and not all builders understand the regulatory or planning

are clad in strips of Welsh hardwood, a material so scanty that it arrived in a blaze of different sizes, hues and grains. The carpenters charged with working with the wood had a natural inclination to systematise it, to alternate the dark and light tones, for example, or to gradually move from the larger strips to the smaller ones. The architects, however, insisted the carpenters approach their work much like the builders of dry stone walls – that is, to grab the first piece of material that comes to hand and make it work. The carpenters feared a hotchpotch but did the architects' bidding. The architects were right: the complete randomness of the Millennium Centre's timber cladding is one of the building's finest features. Sometimes, with a building that aspires to be something beyond the ordinary, the architect needs to be hovering in the shadows. It is important to note though, that the architect should not be allowed to dominate the project. They don't have to live in the finished project, you do. The architect–client relationship needs to be one of partnership therefore, which is a fairly odd position for a professional person to find themself in. 'Houses are different from other purchases, and a client's relationship with an architect is unusual,' says architect and cabinet-maker John Griffiths, 'Architects are dealing with people who aren't professionals, but they're telling you what to do and how they want things to be. There are some things you just can't force on people, and sometimes you just have to eat humble pie.'

Up to this point (the architect's production of the Letter of Agreement), the client has parted with no money and made no firm commitments. It is a frustrating part of an architect's life that they can devote many hours responding to an enquiry, meeting the client, pitching for the work, trying to understand and help formulate the brief, explaining their working methods and perhaps even sketching out ideas, only to be quietly dropped. It is also frustrating when clients remain committed

consequences of making a small change here and there. Moreover, many architects really do agonise over the details, and the precise specification of materials. The manner in which the junctions between surfaces are realised can make the difference between a reasonable refurbishment and a work of habitable sculpture. It is the nature of builders to use tried and tested methods when confronted by drawings, which appear to be ambiguous or questionable, but sometimes the architect needs to be present to explain the intention behind the drawing and to insist they carry out the job in spite of their misgivings.

It is not a domestic project by any means, but the interior of the Welsh Millennium Centre in Cardiff is a case in point. The atria of this marvellous building to the project, and to the architect, but (for reasons known only to them) the Letter of Agreement remains unanswered – or answered only after a long delay. This very early stage of the relationship sets the tone for the rest of the project and it is dangerous for questions of integrity, honesty and commitment, to be raised at this point.

Once the architect has been appointed, you need to set aside time to explore your embryonic brief with them. This could be a consultation lasting a few hours to a full day. It is at this point that fees will start to be incurred. Your aspirations for the project need to be tested and challenged, not because the architect is being contrary but because your fundamental assumptions can be proven only if subjected to close scrutiny. A large architecture firm, when asked by a university to build a bigger teaching facility to cope with greater numbers of students, carried out an in-depth analysis, only to find that the client could get away with commissioning a smaller building if it also amended the teaching schedule. That is what testing the brief is about and it is an important part of the process. So if you tell your architect 'We need another bedroom,' do not be surprised if they answer, 'Oh really? Tell me why'. The new bedroom may be needed to accommodate a new baby or an elderly relative, or to function as an occasional guest room or to boost the value of the house. The reason behind the need could easily prompt a radically different design solution.

The brief for a building project must, when eventually finalised, contain a suggestion of priority and emphasis. Total area could be more important than finish; budget may be more pressing than timetable. It will also help the architect if you are able to say which buildings you admire and be able to provide clues about the tone and mood of the imagined project. Domestic building works are much more expressions of the client than commercial ventures.

The architect will then go away and spend a couple of days drawing up design schemes. This is an important moment in the life of the project. It is at this point that the architect could return having captured the spirit of the exercise in a few deft strokes of the pen. However, the architect might have missed the point completely, or may simply have devised an option to give you something to react against – to force you to provide

some concrete answers. Sometimes you all need to ask yourselves if the preceding phases (search, interview, appointment, brief development) were really explicit enough. This is why the brief needs to contain a certain amount of specificity. It can't all be aspirational. The design process is all about testing solutions against need, taking circuitous routes in order to arrive at something that might have been discussed at the outset. There is no such thing as a bad idea, only a bad mismatch between the idea and the brief.

Part 2 – Fees and Contracts

The common perception is that employing an architect is expensive. That is a partial truth, it certainly can be expensive, but the fact is that architects' fees represent only a small proportion of the total build cost. Architects no longer operate a strict fee structure and the amount you pay an architect is up for negotiation. Generally, for domestic projects, architects will charge around 12–15 per cent of the construction cost. This percentage might go down as the total budget goes up, or it might increase for very small budget jobs or a project requiring a solution to very complex problems. Just about everyone who uses an architect believes the fee is justified and the money well spent. Architects often work very hard for their fee and will undertake much of the trouble-shooting that would otherwise be the responsibility of the client.

Fees do not necessarily have to be expressed as percentages though. It is acceptable to pay a flat fee for the work or to pay by the hour. Some clients even come to private arrangements. In one project featured in this book, a capped percentage deal was reached, where the architect was paid an agreed percentage of the build, up to a certain value. If costs rose beyond that value the fee remained the same. For another project featured here, a flat fee was negotiated; the architect's bid and the client's offer differed by £2,000, but rather than meet in the middle the final fee was settled with the toss of a coin. The architect won.

It is also fairly common to mix methods. It wouldn't be unusual, for example, to pay an architect a flat fee (of a few hundred pounds, perhaps), to produce a document containing a brief survey, an interpretation of the brief, design options and recommendations. Also check whether expenses, such as the printing of drawings or travel, will be additional to the fee. Once a way forward has been agreed, both parties can then move on to a percentage contract. Also, it is not untypical to pay a flat fee for the architect to take the designs through the planning system, and then to receive an hourly rate if the clients prefer to manage the build programme themselves, with the architect on call as necessary. All architects will have preferred ways of working and arrangements can usually be made to keep everybody happy.

It is worth noting that paying invoices promptly will work in the client's favour. Architects generally submit invoices once key stages of the project have been completed, and it is unreasonable to expect them to commence work on a new and more advanced phase of the job if they remain unpaid for previous work. Nothing galls an architect more than a client who strikes a very hard bargain and then withholds payments for no good reason, only to spend far greater sums on a luxury bathroom suite.

Architects are not the only professionals to whom fees will be owed. A structural engineer will inevitably make an appearance on the project and the services of other consultants may also be necessary. This book contains more than one example of building works that have required the assistance of independent planning specialists, to help get planning submissions in the best possible state before being submitted to the local authority. Such specialists can be used to scrutinise and advise on the details to ensure that planners can raise no legitimate objections. Right to light experts may also be needed if neighbours raise fears of overshadowing. And then, of course, there may be further unexpected fees if problems are uncovered during building work that were not appreciated at the start of a project, such as underpinning (see Kitchen extension for a terraced house, Highbury, north London, page 108), that requires specialist subcontractors and engineers.

It is surprising where money can be saved, though. Another project featured within these pages involved big changes to a two-storey Victorian extension. The original idea was to demolish the ground floor of this extension and prop the first floor up while a new structure was inserted beneath (see Kitchen extension for a terraced house, Islington, north London, page 80). The contractor, however, advised that demolishing both storeys and rebuilding the upper floor would be cheaper, easier and quicker. In fact, doing it this way meant that the poorly insulated and flimsily built upper floor was replaced by a structure of modern standards.

When negotiating fees with architects, the subject of builder's contracts may also come up. There is a wide range of standard contracts available to clients, covering small projects to large commercial developments. Architects will advise over the most appropriate contract to opt for. One thing to look out for is whether or not builders can be penalised if the work takes longer than promised. There are often good reasons for delays (poor weather being one), but some clients featured in this book have obtained discounts from builders who have been late completing their work (see case studies on pages 80, 88, 118 and 130); the sum paid was calculated by multiplying the number of weeks overdue by the rental value of the property. More importantly, clients must understand that architects do not manage contracts with builders; the client signs contracts with the builders, and it is the client who pays the builder. Architects do not pass on payments. Architects do, however, inspect builders' work on behalf of the client and they will advise clients on what action to take.

All of which makes commissioning and working with an architect sound rather painful. Embarking on, and living through, even a moderate building project can be time-consuming and frustrating. Building is not easy; it is a messy and complex business at the best of times, and any medium-sized extension or significant refurbishment project could well take two years from inception to completion – perhaps longer. This is what investing in design really means. It is not just a financial investment; it is also one of energy, commitment and vision.

opposite **Katerina Hoey and HARTarchitecture, Extension and Refit of a House, Maida Vale, London.** Delays to this large extension and refurbishment project meant the builder had to pay a financial penalty.

Understanding architects'

The drawing is the architect's stock in trade. When executed clearly, clients should be able to navigate their way quickly around a plan, elevation and section of their building project.

Sketches

In any architectural project, the first type of drawings to be encountered will be either sketches or diagrams. There is a skill to sketching, and it shouldn't be so rough that it can barely be deciphered; nor so well executed that it verges on a work of art. In spite of the way that computer-assisted design has changed working practices, many architects can still sketch confidently and clients should expect their architects to be able to convey a sense of three-dimensional space by making simple, expressive marks on a page. Sketches are valuable for communicating the broad intention of the design – they can convey something of the project's spatial arrangement and even be suggestive of the scheme's atmospherics. A good sketch will capture the spirit of a building in a way that carefully measured plans and elevations cannot. This is why

right **The architect's sketch.** This drawing, quickly roughed out during a conversation with the client, begins to capture the spatial arrangement and relationships of the project, along with relative sizes. It is deliberately rough and rapidly executed, but captures some of the spirit and ambition of the development.

drawings

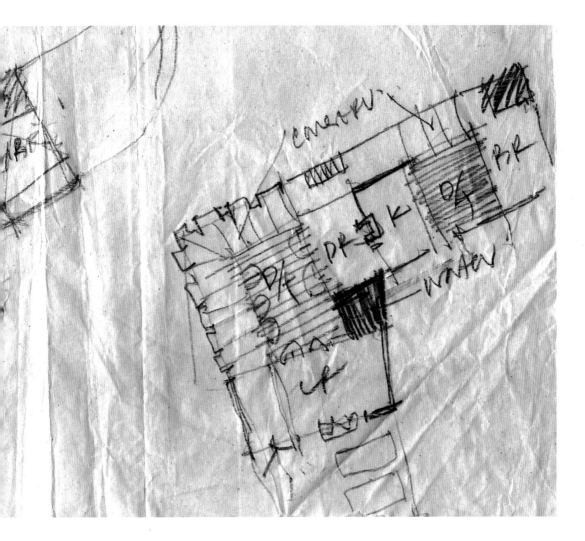

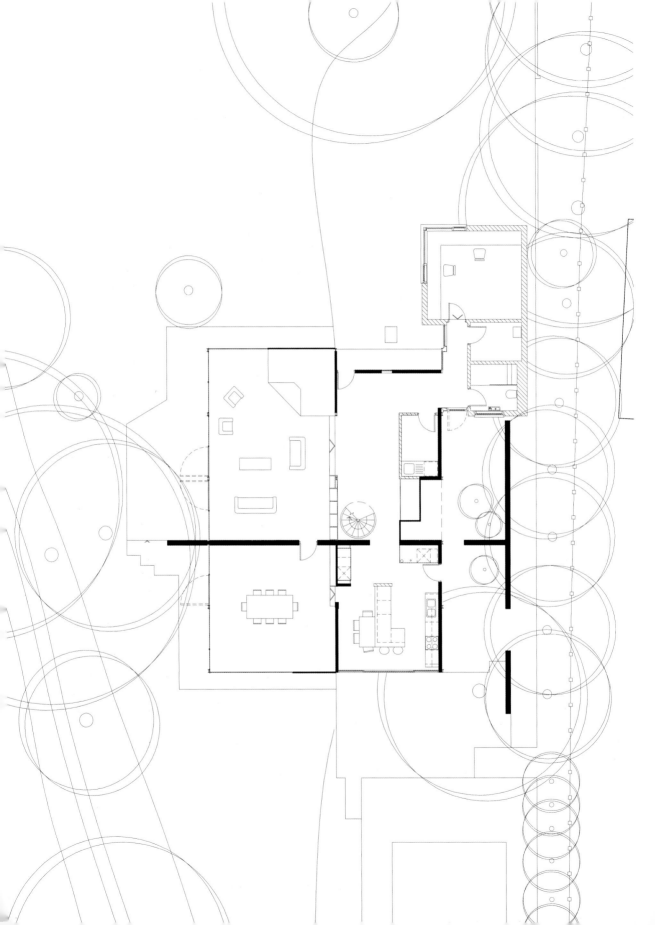

sketches should be kept as an important part of the project archive, no matter how quickly executed and insubstantial they are.

Diagrams

Sketches should not be confused with diagrams, however. Architects like diagrams because they help to compartmentalise ideas and establish broad relationships between key components. A diagram of a house, for example, might bear little resemblance to a real house (in the same way that the London tube map bears little resemblance to the actual paths taken by the tunnels), but it might well include the broad functional requirements and an indication of how they all relate to each other. Functions that need to be kept separate, like a home office and a playroom, would be identified in a diagram. If sketches pay little heed to scale, then diagrams pay even less, but their role cannot be underestimated at the start of any project.

Plans, Sections and Elevations

Eventually, diagrams and sketches become translated into standard architectural drawings – the plans, sections and elevations. These are line drawings that plot precisely all the coordinates of significance. They are flat drawings that may offer little or no indication of depth. Some architects do include blocks of colour to indicate materials. Others add notional shadows, which provide an illusion of depth, but do not confuse these drawings with perspectives. Elevations (drawings of external

walls, with no sense of perspective) are probably the easiest drawings to read – a child's classic rendering of a house (a square decorated with symbols representing a door, windows and chimney) is an elevation. But do remember that, no matter how precisely an elevation has been plotted, you will never see your house like that; when stood in front of a real building, the power of perspective distorts what you see. Elevations occupy a two-dimensional world.

Plans are more complex, but any architect should be capable of generating a plan without the cumbersome technical detail that can make an architectural drawing so forbidding. Typically, floor plans are drawn at about waist height, and they show everything below that point. The best plans will make sensible use of different line thicknesses (or weights) to indicate different features. Imagine taking a chainsaw to your house and slicing through the walls, horizontally. In a plan, thick lines would be used to indicate the cuts made by the chainsaw through the walls; thin lines would be used to indicate features below the cut marks (furniture or the grid of a tiled floor). Glazing should not be indicated with as heavy a line as masonry, while doorways will be indicated by arcs (quarter circles) showing the pivot points. Stairs are indicated by parallel lines, showing stair treads, with an arrow that points upwards. Drawing conventions and protocols vary from practice to practice. Some prefer to use crosshatched lines rather than thick black marks to indicate walls. The important thing is that the conventions are used consistently. Any decent plan, especially of a project as small as a house, should be drawn up in a manner that makes the spatial arrangements obvious.

Sections (or 'cross sections') work in a similar way to plans in that they are slices through a building – only this time they are showing the vertical arrangement of a design, rather than the horizontal arrangement indicated by a plan. Again, thick or shaded lines will tend to indicate where the building has actually been 'cut' while thinner lines are used to show elements that lie in the background, such as doorways and windows. It is important that plans and sections are well coordinated and labelled, enabling quick and easy comparison between the two sets of drawings.

The Axonometric

Architects also have a couple of other drawing types in their armoury. The axonometric, for example, is a plan turned 45 degrees, from which the walls have been projected upwards. This is a useful drawing as it is a sort of combined plan/section/elevation and the image gains a certain three-dimensionality. A similar drawing, called an isometric, does much the same thing. But caution has to be exercised when reading these drawings – very definitely they are not perspective drawings, and measurements should not be taken from them. They can encompass an entire project in a reasonably clear manner and one variation on this drawing type – the 'exploded axonometric' – can be useful because it separates all the elements, allowing the project to be viewed in almost kit form.

above **The computer montage.** This image, based on a computer model, embodies perspective and is just about realistic enough to give a reasonable impression from eye level of what the new building will look like.

Scaled Drawings

One of the most difficult things to appreciate in an architectural drawing is scale. A simple rectangle with no notation or reference to scale is meaningless. There would be no way of knowing if it represents a room, a building, a box or a pixel. Having said that, even with the application of scale, clients can remain mystified. Being told that a rectangle has been drawn to a scale of 1:250 is hardly illuminating. The best way of appreciating scale is by including familiar artefacts such as a car, a washing machine or a human figure within a drawing; that makes a drawing immediately legible. Plans will often include the outline of a kitchen worktop or a toilet bowl, which certainly help to convey a sense of size. It is worth noting that architects will produce drawings to a wide range of scales: a site plan, showing the house in the context of the wider neighbourhood, would typically be 1:500; plans are perfectly legible at 1:100; drawings of details, such as jointing mechanisms or junctions between different materials, might be drawn at 1:20, 1:5, 1:2 or even 1:1 (ie, actual size) depending on the need to specify detail.

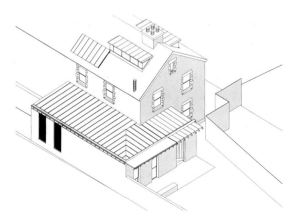

left **The axonometric drawing.** This drawing shows the scheme in three dimensions, and is composed of nothing but diagonals and vertical lines. It is not a perspective drawing, but gives the client a clear idea of what the project involves.

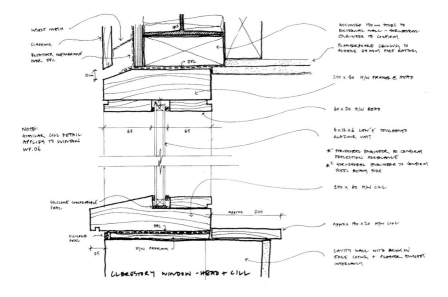

Labels on the detail drawing (top to bottom, left side):

INSECT MESH
CLADDING
BREATHER MEMBRANE OVER DPC
DPC
10mm

NOTE:
SIMILAR SILL DETAIL
APPLIES TO WINDOW
WF.06

65   65

SILICONE COMPRESSIBLE SEAL

SILICONE SEAL

APPROX 200
DPC
H/W PACKING
25

CLERESTORY WINDOW - HEAD + SILL

Labels (right side):

ASSUMED 150mm STUDS TO
EXTERNAL WALL - STRUCTURAL
ENGINEER TO CONFIRM

PLASTERBOARD CEILING TO
ACHIEVE 64 MINS FIRE RATING

240 x 50 H/W FRAME @ HEAD

60 x 20 H/W BEAD

6 x 12 x 6 LOW 'E' TOUGHENED
GLAZING UNIT

*¹ STRUCTURAL ENGINEER TO CONFIRM
DEFLECTION ALLOWANCE
*² STRUCTURAL ENGINEER TO CONFIRM
STEEL BEAM SIZE

240 x 40 H/W SILL

APPROX 130 x 20 H/W SILL

CAVITY WALL WITH BRICK ON
EDGE COPING + PLASTER FINISHES
INTERNALLY

left **The detail drawing.** This sketchy drawing has been compiled for a builder and embodies far more detail than the average client would be interested in. It shows everything from insect mesh to breather membrane, and even contains notes and labels.

Testing the Drawings

There is a peculiar psychology with regard to drawings. Clients can often feel awkward about asking for changes or alternatives, because the drawings look so complete. But no matter how polished and finished they look, especially those generated on a computer, they are only drawings and can therefore be amended. Architects often go to considerable lengths to compile a good, legible and meaningful set of drawings, but they are nothing more than tools of the trade, representations of an idea and nothing more. Even well-executed drawings require the client to exercise their imagination. Clients must try to bring the drawings to life, and inhabit the spaces that are described by them. Walk through the rooms indicated in the drawings; look out of the windows illustrated by fine pencil marks; imagine how sunlight might play upon the walls, and how voices might carry through the house. It is only by testing the drawings and asking tough questions, that the drawings can be proven to contain a workable idea. If the spaces suggested by them are found to be wanting, the drawings must be adjusted.

Equally, clients should be prepared to make their own judgements about the atmospherics of particular drawings. Perspective representations, which purport to show a scheme as it will really look, can, with a few judicious strokes of a pen, appear dynamic and full of life. Make certain that the rules of perspective have not been adjusted for effect, and be aware that shadows rarely behave as shown in charcoal drawings or computer models.

Many architects generate drawings and models digitally. Apart from SketchUp (a powerful 3D modelling program that is either cheap or free, depending on the version) architectural drawing and modelling packages tend to be quite expensive. This does not mean, however, that you have to purchase a licence to open and read a computer-generated drawing.

The world's biggest manufacturer of architectural design software is the US company Autodesk, which produces a program called AutoCAD. Drawings executed in AutoCAD can be opened on a computer via a special free-to-download viewer called Autodesk Design Review. Drawings can be saved as PDFs, the universal file exchange format, and opened in Adobe Reader.

SketchUp is owned by Google, which means that users can easily export a model of their home to GoogleEarth.

Space and style

So what is space? In architectural terms, space is about much more than square metres or cubic feet. Any architectural space, and especially one that functions as a home, embraces texture, light, sound and colour – very probably smell too. Architects can, of course, steer you on a course for extra space but they should also be able to make that space sing. Rooms can be lofty presentation pieces or cosy snugs; natural light can wash across wall surfaces or artificial light can pick out precise details; they can be colourful or white abstract spaces against which possessions like furniture and books sit boldly. These are just some of the considerations, simultaneously poetic and practical, through which clients have to wade.

These issues are just as pertinent for people who want to extend or remodel their homes, as opposed to building from scratch. In fact, additions to existing buildings can make architects and clients think particularly hard because there is a context to respond to. This is not about 'fitting in', because the existing building merely sets the tone for an extension – it does not dictate exactly how the job should be done. Brick houses need not be extended with brick (timber may suffice). The composition and size of the development are just as important as the building material. As this book demonstrates, Victorian houses can be effectively extended with flat-roofed structures that make little or no reference to the original buildings. Inside, though,

the join between house and extension is less clear. Generally, an architectural project bleeds through the house, blurring the distinction between old and new. Serious architectural works rarely limit themselves to adding a distinct new room, entirely separate from the rest of the house; instead, whole chunks of the house, even the ways the inhabitants live their lives, can become reinvented. Junctions between new and old are created forcing homeowners to re-examine much that surrounds them (flooring materials, decorative elements, the grain of wood) as well as how they actually move around the house.

Sound is probably one of the factors least considered when planning spaces. Yet it is crucial to how one experiences a building. Hard and soft surfaces cannot be specified without being at least mildly aware of their acoustic properties. Will you click-clack across a polished concrete floor on sharp heels, or drift barefoot over the slight springiness of timber boards? Will music be played? Sound bounces off hard surfaces, so

opposite Space is more than just square footage, or cubic metres. Space involves colour, texture, light, views and even smell.

a music lover might want to reconsider that space of steel, glass and resin. This explains why even the most contemporary of performance halls are loaded with textures and soft furnishings – calculations are even made about the ways that the audience itself will deflect and absorb the sounds that are being played. Sound, then, feels comfortable around fabric, sofas, rugs and carpets.

Likewise, people often forget the importance of touch. It is a real oddity, but it's remarkable how little we actually touch our buildings – when we do touch them, we touch them a lot. Door handles, light switches, the opening mechanisms of windows, taps, doorbells … the palms of your hands and your finger tips will tell you a lot about the quality of a place. If a house is built to feel solid (with all the practical and psychological guarantees of safety that solidity implies) the quality of the ironmongery is no less significant than the weight of the masonry or steel from which the house is built.

The point of this essay is to demonstrate that building projects, if they are to be truly successful, need to be thought through to almost ridiculous degrees. Views are a good example of this. It is plainly a good idea to frame a fine view if one is available. But how good is it really? Capturing the verdant trees at the bottom of your garden is all well and good in the summer, but a winter view might reveal something else entirely. Similarly, you need to know exactly how you will gaze at your view. There is nothing more galling than a wonderful vista that disappears when you sit down, because the sill has been set too high. If you plan to lie in bed and contemplate the scene outside your window, the architect needs to know the height of your bed.

When planning your space you also have to dream your way through it – to switch on the virtual reality of your imagination and tour your reinvented home in 3D. There comes a point in all projects when you have to stop looking at the project in plan and interrogate it as if you are actually in the space itself, looking at it in perspective, noticing everything and checking all is well. Too often, spaces become resolved in plan only (that is, from above), which means that thickness and depth become forgotten. None of this is really about style; it is about rigour and robust thinking. It doesn't really matter what design language, or materials palette, you choose so long as everything has been considered and the thousands of elements within every project have a degree of coherence. This is the difference between taking a purely visual approach to a project and an experiential one. Some architectural thinkers believe that too often buildings are designed purely for visual effect and that other senses (touch, hearing) are ignored. Architecture, the thinking goes, is coming to be conceived almost photographically, entire buildings are designed around key views and surface effects. There is a lot of truth to this critique, and the point here is to stress that homes are not merely for looking at but living in. Hovering just behind the questions, 'how much space do you want?' and 'what does your new project look like?' is the far more important query, 'how do you want to feel in your home?'

And then there is the big idea. Of course, most domestic clients do not give their projects a theoretical underpinning, but many will have a value system that puts a premium on, for example, sustainability, a relationship with landscape, flexibility or colour. These values might drive a project, or at least fuel its development. It is important to retain some sense of these ideas or principles throughout the project – not necessarily to be dominated by them, but certainly not to abandon them. Efforts at sustainability, for example, do not necessarily mean photo-voltaics and grey water recycling. A project that embraces sustainable thinking could simply be super-insulated to keep heating bills down (heating and powering buildings is one of the largest contributors to CO_2 emissions), or to use recycled or recyclable materials. An overriding idea might also be one of design language, especially if a client wants to counterpoint an elderly house with a crisp modern addition. 'Minimalism' is a term that probably applies here, although there are plenty of signs that a strict interpretation of this pared-back movement is on the wane. The irony about Minimalism is that it is

opposite **Griffiths Gottschalk, Modernisation of a Country Cottage, Wiltshire.** What do you want your space to sound like? Will you click-clack across a polished concrete floor on sharp heels, or drift barefoot over the slight springiness of timber boards? Will music be played?

rarely cheap; design composed of what look like just a few deft moves can be spectacularly expensive. This is due mainly to the care with which these spaces have to be assembled. There is no room for error, and Minimalist interiors that live up to the idea require good quality builders and fine materials. Corners and edges have to be executed perfectly and they need to be kept that way. However, there are one or two details from this hyper-Modernist design language that translate well to less onerous design solutions. One of them is the shadow gap. Shadow gaps make it possible to make different surfaces meet satisfactorily by not quite meeting – there is a gap, in shadow. This detail elegantly gets around the difficult issue of making perfect junctions, especially if those junctions are the meeting points of different materials. They are the opposite of complex mouldings, and do the job just as well. They are almost like deliberate cracks.

This is not the place to dive into the awkward territory of style. Style is too bound up with taste and fashion for rights and wrongs to apply. What is appropriate is far more important than matters of style. Consider, also, that style is often bound up with what is important to a particular culture. There can be powerful ideas and very specific ways of looking at the world lying behind what we call decoration. Take Gothic, for example. Gothic designs, which were reprised so spectacularly in the 19th century, were not reintroduced to British culture simply because popular taste changed; it was hardly a simple matter of preferring the pointed arch to the rounded one. Gothic architecture, in an age where industrialisation was transforming both towns and countryside, was reintroduced as a way of remembering the past – it was seen as a convincing (largely English) design language that went hand in hand with Arthurian

legend, with a golden age, which preceded the rationalist Enlightenment (characterised by classical architecture, representative of Greek, Roman and Italian Renaissance thought). At a time when factory-made products threatened the livelihoods of craftsmen, thinkers began to look back to the construction of the great cathedrals and the collective endeavour of skilled people in the service of God. Gothic designs made people feel comfortable and gave them a sense of continuity with the past. In spite of the upheaval, the nation was still in touch with its roots. That was the theory anyway, and the new Gothic was often controversial; the fantastical Midland Hotel, stuck to the front of the very practical engineering triumph of the train shed at St Pancras station, was criticised for its backward-looking aesthetic. One critic asked whether railway staff should wear medieval dress. In fact, much earlier than the Victorian era, Christopher Wren came under some pressure to cap the new St Paul's cathedral with a spire rather than a dome – domes were considered a bit too Italian, and therefore Catholic, to some late 17th century churchgoers. Wren, obviously, ignored them.

The point of this very brief history lesson is that design movements very often have intellectual, cultural and historical theories propping them up. They emerge in response to something else. They aren't just patterns; they are symbols. Property developers would do well, therefore, to understand what they're doing when they make their choices. Designs can be expressive of their age, and they reveal a lot about the people who commission them. Part of the decision-making process with regard to design language is also a response to context. Being contextual, however, does not necessarily mean creating a slavish copy of an existing building

– an intelligent and sensitive response to a site could have something to do with proportion, scale, geometric rhythm, materials and style. Sometimes an architectural acknowledgement of just one of these things will suffice, creating a sense of design continuity in a subtle way. In conservation areas, which are set up to 'preserve or enhance' the 'character and appearance' of a neighbourhood, planners will probably expect a deeper and more considered understanding of context without necessarily resorting to mimicry or pastiche. The same applies to listed buildings. Occasionally, a counterpoint to the original building, where juxtaposition is celebrated, can be appropriate so long as it is handled deftly rather than clumsily. Bear in mind also that the use of glass, a material beloved of architecture students for its transparency and ability to make large enclosures 'disappear', doesn't always behave as anticipated; glass, depending on the ways that light plays upon it, can appear highly reflective, metallic and incredibly solid.

Design language (or style) is bound closely with materials. The truth is, almost anything is possible provided you have the budget for it, and there is a material available for almost any job. Glass, for example, can now be used structurally, and can be coated in layers, which allow light to penetrate, while keeping the heat out (allowing large south-facing spans). Engineered timber (such as glued laminated timber called 'glulam') has been developed to span large spaces effortlessly. Corten steel develops a fine coating of protective rust, and therefore a deep red/brown colour, while copper products include panels that gradually go green, due to the natural patina which occurs under weathering, or maintain their brown colour. Some copper products even appear gold. Even concrete, which has suffered from an image problem due to many developments in the sixties and seventies, is undergoing something of a rehabilitation. Very white concretes are available and some architects have experimented with adding extra

ingredients to the aggregate, which add a sparkle to the finished product. The most interesting projects are often those that employ a mix of contemporary and traditional materials, or use old materials in new and interesting ways. Some projects featured in this book use both oak and stainless steel; another clads a garden lock-up in mirrored glass. Others even employ 'green roofs', that is, roofs which are seeded and flourish as grass or wildflowers. As well as being prettier to look down upon, green roofs have excellent insulative properties.

It is tempting to say that good quality materials must be used at all times – but that just isn't true. Again, that word 'appropriate' applies. This book contains numerous examples of clients who have spent their money in a discriminatory way, where savings have been made in some quarters only to be invested in others. It has become almost standard practice to use IKEA kitchen carcasses paired with bespoke doors and worktops, and there is nothing wrong with that. Polycarbonate, cheaply available from DIY stores, is used in a finely tuned apartment development in east London, described in this book (see Creation of an apartment on a warehouse roof, Shoreditch, east London, page 150), while breezeblocks are part of a palette of materials including oak and Indian slate, also described in these pages (see Transformation of a farm building, Somerset, page 14). Other projects use paving slabs – more usually associated with patios – in the kitchen (and you would never know). Plywood is also a relatively cheap material, much loved by many architects today, that can be used just as effectively as expensive hardwoods. Similarly, worktops can be cast from concrete as well as expensive but wonderful Corian.

Architectural projects are multidimensional in much more than a spatial sense. They operate on levels that include dreaming, budgeting, time management and craft. Striking a balance between all these elements is the hardest thing of all – but that is what has made all the case studies in this book so satisfying and so successful.

left It is remarkable how little we touch our homes. But when we do touch them (via items such as taps, switches and door knobs) we touch them a lot.

Glossary

Architects Registration Board (ARB)
Architects benefit from 'protection of title', which means that no one is allowed to call themselves an architect unless they meet the terms set out by, and policed by, the Architects Registration Board. Anyone calling themself an architect who is not listed by the ARB is acting illegally.

Arts and Crafts
A late 19th-century movement in England which encouraged craftsmanship and an appreciation of history and vernacular architecture. Gothic and picturesque elements were used in the design of housing. Key figures associated with this movement are William Morris, Philip Webb and WR Lethaby.

Beam
A horizontal structural element, usually of timber or steel. (Incidentally, our modern use of the word 'beam' is probably derived from the Anglo–Saxon word for tree.)

Breather Membrane
Breather membranes are found in roof and wall structures (especially timber-wall structures). They are specially formulated to allow moisture to pass from the inside to the outside, but to prevent water from passing from the outside to the inside. This keeps the interior of the house dry and free of damp.

Building Regulations
As well as requiring planning permission, new buildings must adhere to the terms of a wide range of building regulations covering energy performance, safety and the technical standard of the building work. Building regulation approval and planning permission are applied for separately.

Cavity Wall
A wall comprising an inner and outer surface, with a space (the cavity) between. It is intended to improve the insulative property of the wall and reduce damp. Increasingly, the cavity is filled with insulation rather than left as a void.

The care with which this kitchen was planned and put together is impressive. The project is an exercise in exactness, while a plentiful supply of cupboard space allows the surfaces to remain free of clutter.

Contemporary design need not always turn its back on tradition and craft. Clean lines, simplicity and the careful articulation of different materials create a refreshing interpretation of a very ordinary household feature.

Classical

Architectural style based on the principles of Greek and Roman architecture, based on the study of ancient ruins, developed during and since the Renaissance period.

Composition

Architects and artists will use the term 'composition' to describe the arrangement and balance of shapes and lines in a design. The composition might be guided by a strict adherence to a grid of imaginary lines, or a standard formula such as the Golden Section. Or it might simply be a matter of personal judgement.

Conservation Areas

Areas deemed to be of special architectural or historic interest, the character or appearance of which it is desirable to preserve or enhance.

Contracts

There are a wide range of standard contracts available to clients, covering even small works. Architects will advise on the most appropriate contract. Significantly, architects do not sign contracts with builders (contractors) on behalf of clients. Clients sign contracts direct with the builder. Likewise, clients pay the contractor directly. Architects will, however, inspect building works on behalf of clients, and can advise the client about whether or not the terms of the builder's contract are being fulfilled.

Contractor

The main builder contracted to undertake the principal building work on a project.

Damp-proof Course/Membrane

All buildings built to modern standards will have a damp-proof course (DPC), which prevents moisture rising from ground level. Traditionally, this level was created from a single layer of special brick or slate being incorporated into the wall. Today, sheets of plastic tend to be used instead – the damp-proof membrane (or DPM). DPCs should be raised above ground level, otherwise splashing from rain or mild flooding will create damp above the course.

Designer

Homeowners do not always need the services of an architect to reinvent their home – the services of an "architectural designer" or "interior designer" may be appropriate. These titles are not protected by law (unlike the term "architect") so you will have to ask careful questions to check that a designer genuinely is up to the job. Really good interior designers can have a much more developed sense of space, materials and detailing than architects – but interior designers can also be little more than soft furnishings enthusiasts and furniture specifiers.

Elevation

The facade of a building or a drawing depicting the facade.

Gable Wall

A gable wall marks the ends of a pitched roof (a sloping roof of two inclines, forming an inverted 'V'). The gable wall may sit beneath an overhanging roof, or may rise above it, forming a parapet.

Joist

Horizontal timber spanning the space between walls and beams, on which floors and ceilings are supported.

Lintel

The beam over an opening, such as a door or window, which supports the weight of the wall above.

Low-emissivity Glass

Glass with an invisible coating to control the transfer of heat. Coatings can be applied to the outside of the glass, keeping out the heat of the sun; or to the inside, preventing the heat of the house from escaping.

Modernism

A broad cultural movement, originating in the 1920s, which affected architecture greatly– largely in Continental Europe. The movement dispensed with ornament and strived for an industrial aesthetic, typified by flat roofs, strip-windows (elongated, rectangular windows) in metal frames, flat planes, gentle curves and whiteness. Post-Modernism was a term coined to mark a move away from this aesthetic in the 1980s, when historical references (such as pediments) began to be self-consciously applied to new buildings.

Mullion

The vertical post between plates of glass in a window.

Outline Plan of Work

The RIBA publishes an 'Outline Plan of Work', which describes the sequence of stages under which an architect manages a contract and client relationship. Stages progress from stage A to stage L and cover matters such as identification of client need, implementation of design brief, administration of building contract, and final inspections.

Overlooking

This applies when a building development risks providing views of areas that people would rather remain private. A single-storey extension topped by a roof garden or balcony could offer the occupants intrusive views into a neighbour's garden, for example. Such issues will be dealt with at the planning stage.

Elevation for a two storey extension to an 18th century cottage in Bristol. The scheme, by architect Nigel Bedford, includes a double garage and garden room.

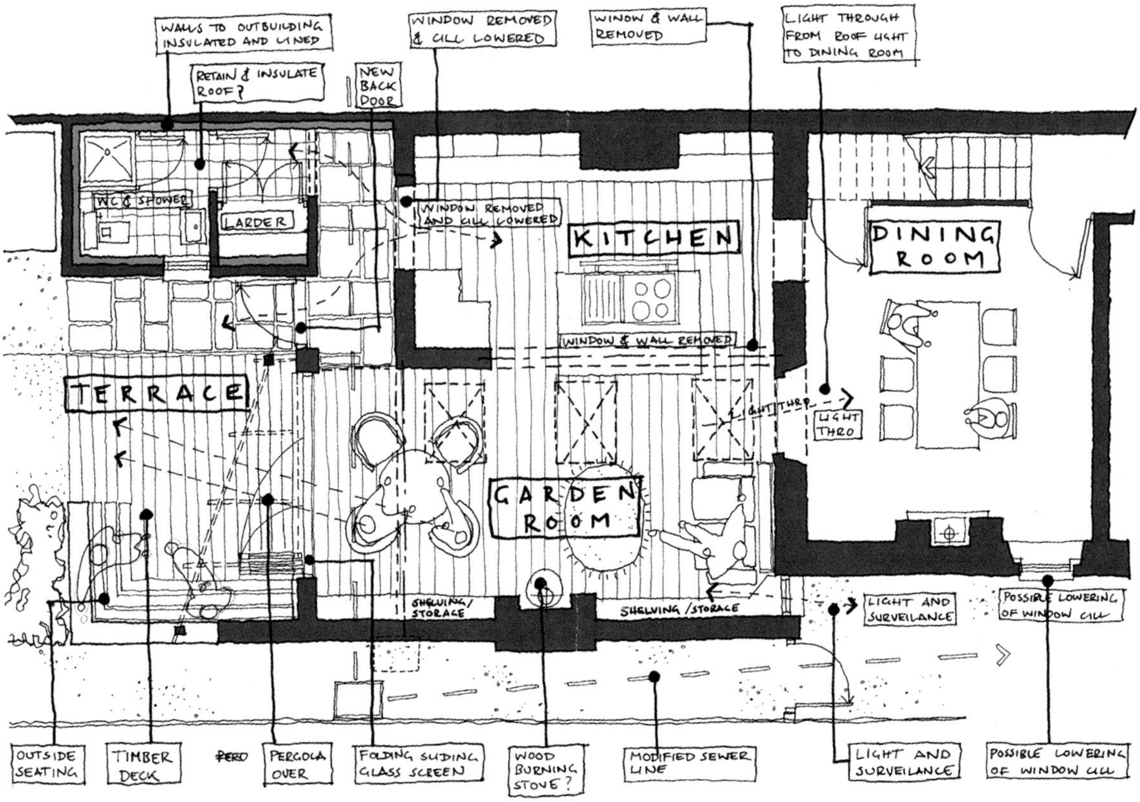
WALLS TO OUTBUILDING INSULATED AND LINED
RETAIN & INSULATE ROOF?
NEW BACK DOOR
WINDOW REMOVED & CILL LOWERED
WINOW & WALL REMOVED
LIGHT THROUGH FROM ROOF LIGHT TO DINING ROOM
WC & SHOWER
LARDER
WINDOW REMOVED AND CILL LOWERED
KITCHEN
DINING ROOM
WINDOW & WALL REMOVED
TERRACE
LIGHT THRO
GARDEN ROOM
SHELVING/STORAGE
SHELVING/STORAGE
LIGHT AND SURVEILANCE
POSSIBLE LOWERING OF WINDOW CILL
OUTSIDE SEATING
TIMBER DECK
PERGOLA OVER
FOLDING SLIDING GLASS SCREEN
WOOD BURNING STOVE?
MODIFIED SEWER LINE
LIGHT AND SURVEILANCE
POSSIBLE LOWERING OF WINDOW CILL

Plan, with detailed notes, for a kitchen/breakfast/garden room extension to a Victorian semi-detached house. The plan, by architect Nigel Bedford for a house in Wiltshire, also converts an external store into a utility/WC

Party Wall Agreement

Party walls are those walls which separate (but are shared by) adjoining properties, such as those in a terrace. Homeowners proposing to do work that affects the party wall are obliged to consult with their neighbour and secure their agreement under the terms of the Party Wall etc. Act 1996. The government publishes a free guide to the Act (product code 02 BR 00862).

Permitted Development Rights

Homeowners are often allowed to carry out limited forms of development, including extensions, without the need to make an application to a local planning authority, under the terms of the Town and Country Planning (General Permitted Development) Order. Additions are generally limited to single-storey developments. It is always worth checking with your local authority about whether your plans are covered by permitted development rights, or whether full planning permission is required. Permitted development may not apply (or may be curtailed) in conservation areas.

Plan

A horizontal section through a building, showing how the rooms are arranged.

Planning Permission

Formal approval sought from a council, often granted with conditions, allowing a proposed development to proceed. Permission may be sought in principle through outline planning applications, or be sought in detail through full planning applications.

Right to Light

Neighbours, who fear that a building project will overshadow their own property, or reduce the amount of light they have grown accustomed to, can make a case under 'right to light' rules. However, this does not mean that light cannot be reduced at all; instead, it means that properties should benefit from a certain amount of light. Specialists using strict calculations, often backed up by computer programs, will undertake assessments to ensure neighbours' rights to light are not infringed.

Royal Institute of British Architects (RIBA)

The RIBA is a representative body for the architecture profession and membership is voluntary (unlike the Architects Registration Board, which charges an annual registration fee to anyone who wishes to practice as an architect). The RIBA exists to promote architecture and architects, and is a good source of information for people wishing to embark on an architectural project.

Rustication

Deliberately roughened stone, as opposed to smooth-faced stone (known as ashlar).

Section

A vertical cut through a building showing the structure behind the elevation.

Sketch Model

A rough, quickly made model demonstrating the fundamental ideas and spaces behind a proposed design solution. The three-dimensional equivalent of a drawn sketch, sketch models are invaluable design tools and should not be underestimated.

Subcontractor

Building specialists who work under the direction of the principal contractor. Subcontractors are typically trades such as electricians, plumbers and plasterers, or people used to install specialist products, for example, a zinc roof or a wood-burning stove.

Threshold

Architects often use the term "threshold" in the context of "door". This is not to be merely verbose, however. The term implies something of an experience, a passing from one environment (for example, the outside) to another (the inside). Thresholds are transitional spaces. It is a useful term, if not over used.

Transom

Horizontal element separating plates of glass in a window.

Truss

A rigid framework composed of timber or metal, which spans a space – typically to support the roof. In strictly engineering terms, trusses perform the same function as beams.

Underpinning

Buildings that have moved or suffer from subsidence may require underpinning to strengthen their foundations. This requires excavating soil and perhaps part of the existing foundation, and replacement with a deeper, stronger foundation of (typically) concrete and steel. This procedure must be carried out to the specification of an engineer.

Vernacular

Vernacular is a term applied to buildings that have been constructed simply and from local materials and methods – and often without the help of architects. They express the traditions of their local community. Agricultural buildings and cottages are good examples of vernacular buildings.

The old and the new. Victorian mouldings were retained and repaired in this extension and refurbishment project. High quality materials and an attention to detail creates a fine blend of the original house and 21st century tastes.

Directory

Architects featured in this book

Alastair Howe Architects
Parndon Mill
Parndon Mill Lane
Harlow
CM20 2HP
01279 439640
www.alastairhowe.co.uk

Barbara Weiss Architects
16A Crane Grove
London N7 8LE
020 7609 1867
bw@barbaraweissarchitects.com
www.barbaraweissarchitects.com

CaSA Architects
Attika Workspace
Bath Brewery
Toll Bridge Road
Bath
BA1 7DE
01225 851871
studio@casa-architects.com
www.casa-architects.co.uk/

Charlotte Skene Catling
44 Lexington Street
London W1F 0LW
0207 287 0771
contact@charlotteskenecatling.com
www.charlotteskenecatling.com/

Form Design Architecture
1 Bermondsey Exchange,
179–181 Bermondsey St.
London SE1 3UW
020 7407 3336
www.form-architecture.co.uk/

Gledhill Walker Architects
Attika Workspace
Bath Brewery
Toll Bridge Road
Bath
BA1 7DE
01225 851870
martin@gledhillwalker.com

Griffiths Gottschalk
griffiths.gottschalk@yahoo.co.uk

HARTarchitecture
34a Digby Crescent
London N4 2HR
020 8802 8896
th@hartarchitecture.co.uk

Hallett Pollard Hilliar
1A Prior Park Rd
Bath
BA2 4NG
01225 471773
www.hphltd.co.uk/

Optimising space: this neat little desk has been cleverly incorporated into a new kitchen without compromising the aesthetics of the project.

Suppliers and Key Agencies

Platform
1–3 Farman Street
Brighton
BN3 1AL
01273 723 322
www.platformgroup.co.uk

Scape Architects
Unit 2
Providence Yard
Off Ezra Street
London E2 7RJ
020 7012 1244
mail@scape-architects.com
www.scape-architects.com

Spratley Studios
Isis House
43 Station Road
Henley-on-Thames
RG19 1AG
01491 411277
www.spratley.co.uk

David Thurlow Partnership
The Studio
2a Church Lane
Limpley Stoke
Bath BA2 7GH
01225 720114
dt@davidthurlowconsultancy.co.uk

Tonkin Liu
24 Rosebery Avenue
London EC1 4SX
020 78376255
mail@tonkinliu.co.uk
www.tonkinliu.co.uk/

London Basement Company
Innovation House
292 Worton Road
Isleworth
TW7 6EL
www.tlbc.co.uk
Tel: 0208 847 9449
Fax: 0208 380 4999

Whicharchitect.com
4.10 Clerkenwell Workshops
27/31 Clerkenwell Close
London
EC1R 0AT
0870 8966119
Email: info@whicharchitect.com
www.whicharchitect.com

Architectyourhome
www.architect-yourhome.com/
0800 849 8505

Royal Australian Institute of Architects
National Office
Level 2, 7 National Circuit
BARTON ACT 2600
PO Box 3373
MANUKA ACT 2603
(02) 6121 2000
national@raia.com.au
www.architecture.com.au

Royal Institute of British Architects (RIBA)
www.architecture.com
020 7580 5533

RIBA East

The Studio,
High Green,
Great Shelford,
Cambridge
CB22 5EG
Tel: 01223 566285
Fax: 01223 505142
riba.east@inst.riba.org

RIBA East Midlands

Art, Architecture and Design
University of Lincoln
Lincoln
LN6 7TS
01522 837480
riba.eastmidlands@inst.riba.org

RIBA London

66 Portland Place,
London W1B 1AD
020 7307 3681
 riba.london@inst.riba.org
riba.london@inst.riba.org

RIBA North East

The School of the Built Environment
University of Northumbria
Ellison Building
Ellison Place
Newcastle upon Tyne
NE1 8ST
0191 222 0186
riba.northeast@inst.riba.org

RIBA North West

RENEW Rooms
82 Wood Street
Liverpool
L1 4DQ
0151 703 0107
riba.northwest@inst.riba.org

RIBA South

2A The Stables
Sandford Farm
Woodley, Reading
RG5 4SU
0118 969 8051
riba.south@inst.riba.org

RIBA South East

17 Upper Grosvenor Road
Tunbridge Wells
Kent TN1 2DU
01892 515878
info@ribasoutheast.org

RIBA South West

PO Box 72
Budleigh Salterton
Devon
EX9 7WY
0844 800 2767/01395 445096
riba.southwest@inst.riba.org

RIBA Wessex

12c Church Farm
Business Park, Corston
Bath BA2 9AP
0844 800 2767
riba.wessex@inst.riba.org

RIBA West Midlands

Birmingham & Midland Institute,
Margaret Street,
Birmingham
B3 3SP
0121 233 2321
riba.westmidlands@inst.riba.org

RIBA Yorkshire

The Green Sand Foundry
99 Water Lane
Holbeck
Leeds
LS11 5QN
0113 237 8480
riba.yorkshire@inst.riba.org

RIBA Bookshop

RIBA Bookshops (Mail Order Office),
15 Bonhill Street
London
EC2P 2EA
020 7256 7222
sales@ribabookshops.com
www.ribabookshops.com

Royal Society of Architects in Wales/ Cymdeithas Frenhinol Penseiri yng Nghymru (RSAW)

Bute Building
King Edward VII Avenue
Cathays Park
Cardiff
CF10 3NB
029 2087 4753
rsaw@inst.riba.org

Royal Society of Ulster Architects

2 Mount Charles
Belfast
BT7 1NZ
028 9032 3760
028 9023 7313
info@rsua.org.uk
www.rias.org.uk

The Royal Incorporation of Architects in Scotland

15 Rutland Square
Edinburgh Scotland
EH12BE
0131 229 7545
info@rias.org.uk
www.rias.org.uk

The American Institute of Architects

1735 New York Ave., NW
Washington, DC 20006-5292
800-AIA-3837 or 202-626-7300
infocentral@aia.org
www.aia.org

Architects Registration Board

020 7580 5861
info@arb.org.uk
www.arb.org.uk

Building Centre

0207 692 4000
www.buildingcentre.co.uk

Concrete Centre

www.concretecentre.com

100% Design, annual contemporary design show

www.100percentdesign.co.uk

Walter Segal Self Build Trust

www.segalselfbuild.co.uk

Singapore Institute of Architects

79B Neil Road
Singapore 088904
6226 2668
info@sia.org.sg
www.sia.org.sg

Too often contemporary design is concerned with featureless surfaces and flatness. This textured wall creates a depth that is unusual in domestic interiors.

Picture credits

The author and the publisher gratefully acknowledge the people who gave their permission to reproduce material in the book. While every effort has been made to contact copyright holders for their permission to reprint material the publishers would be grateful to hear from any copyright holder who is not acknowledged here and will undertake to rectify any errors or omissions in future editions.

Front cover image © Gareth Gardner. Back cover image © James Morris. Back cover inset images, top to bottom (1) © James Morris, (2, 3, 4, 5) © Gareth Gardner, (6) Photographer Edmund Sumner, Plastik Architects, © View Pictures.

Photographs pp 6-7 (l to r images 1, 4, 6), 13 (t r), 26, 28, 30, 31, 32, 33, 161 © Sebastian Lomas; drawings and sketches pp 35, 165, 176 © Alastair Howe Architects; photographs pp 42, 44-9 © Piers Awdry; drawings and sketches pp 90-1, 94 (t), 159 (t r), 174-5, 177-8 © The David Thurlow Partnership; photographs pp 1, 5, 6 (l to r images 2, 3, 6), 10, 11 (t), 12, 13 (b, l), 56, 59-69, 71 (t l, m, r), 88, 92-3, 94 (b), 95-8, 100-3, 105-7, 108, 110, 112-14, 116-18, 120-21, 123-27, 129 (b l), 138, 140-43, 158, 167, 170, 173, 181-82, 185-86, 189, 193, 195, 198, 199 ((t r, b l) © Gareth Gardner; photographs pp 70, 71 (b r), 72, 74, 75-9, 159 (t l), 168-9 photographer Edmund Sumner, architects The Pike Practice, © View Pictures; photographs 71 (b l), 80, 83, 84, 86 photographer Edmund Sumner, architects Plastik Architects, © View Pictures; drawings and sketches pp 82, 85, 179 © Plastik Architects; drawings and sketches pp 17, 18 © Skene Catling De La Pena; photographs pp 1 (t), 6 (l to r images 5,8), 11 (b), 13 (t l, m), 14, 16, 17 (b), 19-25, 199 (b r) © James Morris; drawings and sketches p 38 © CaSA Architects; photographs pp 36, 39-41, 199 (m l) © Adam Dennes and Piers Awdry; drawings and sketches pp 46-7 © Martin Gledhill; photographs pp 8, 13 (b r), 50, 52-5, 199 (t l) © Photography Darren Chung; drawings and sketches p 52 © Spratley Studios; drawings and sketches p 58 © Hallett Pollard Hilliar; drawings and sketches p 74 © The Pike Practice; drawings and sketches p 104 © Chris Jones/Jones Associates; drawings and sketches pp 111-12 © Prewett Bizley Architects; drawings and sketches p 122 © HARTarchitecture; drawings and sketches pp 132-3 © Scape Architects; photographs pp 3, 128-30, 134-7, 188 © kilian@light-room; photographs pp 129 (t r), 144, 146-7, 149 © Bruce Hemming Photography; drawings and sketches pp 152, 154 © Tonkin Liu; photographs pp 2, 129 (t l, b m), 150, 153, 155-7 photographer Richard Bryant, Tonkin Liu Architects © Arcaid 2008; photographs pp 190-191 © Atelier 17 Ltd.